THE FERGUSON
DILEMMA

Healing America's Racial Wounds

Jade Lee

CONVERGENCE
MOVEMENT

a product of Convergence Movement
Marietta, GA

Convergence Movement

The Ferguson Dilemma
©2017 by Jade Lee

This title is also available online at: ConvergenceMovement.com and JadeLee.org

Request for information should be addressed to: info@jadelee.org

Printed in the United States of America.

ISBN: 978-1-946917-02-7

Published by International Publishing Inc.

1208 N. Centerville Turnpike
Chesapeake, VA 23320

To Convergence Movement
Integrating Cultures in Hard Spaces

Contents

What is The Ferguson Dilemma?

On August 9th, 2014 a 18 year old unarmed African American man named Michael Brown was fatally shot by a 28 year old white police officer named Darren Wilson in Ferguson, MO. Ferguson, a suburb of St. Louis, MO is a predominantly black town with predominantly white police officers and a history of racial tension. The basis of much of this tension is said to be surrounding injustices towards African Americans propagated by white police officers and the Ferguson justice department. On August 9th, 2014, the black people of Ferguson had enough.

Upon the news of the shooting Ferguson erupted with violence and protest to the shock and astonishment of an America who thought she was far past the racial wounds of yesteryear. Ferguson, demonstrated that while we have made progress in this great nation, there are still many racial wounds that must be addressed in order for America to be fully healed, and fully whole.

This book The Ferguson Dilemma, Healing America's Racial Wounds is not a detailed account of the Michael Brown shooting, the events following, nor the recent history of the tensions leading up to this event. Rather, this book will take us to the root of what happened on that tragic day and illustrate the greater Ferguson Dilemma that is present in cities and towns across this nation. As you read this

book you will gain a deeper understanding of the unhealed pain o
people who continue to face systematic oppression on a daily bas
The problem in Ferguson MO is multiplied in many other tow
with names other than Ferguson, but Ferguson will be the flashpoi
used to tell the untold stories of many unnamed Michael Brown's.

This is *The Ferguson Dilemma*.
Corey Lee, Pastor
Convergence Church & Movement

Foreword

Get ready to be challenged ! This is no "book as usual ". With personal vulnerability and well researched content , Jade brings a challenge to every reader of any race , background or persuasion. You think you've got racism " figured out " , think again. Since understanding is the beginning of wisdom , this thoughtful work will both broaden and deepen your understanding of the persuasive "downstream" symptoms of racism that still grip our world. Read this compelling work with an open mind and heart and you'll gain practical wisdom for intentional steps you can take as a healer and peacemaker.

Decades after Reverend Martin Luther King Jr's March on Washington , the wounds of racial injustice remain unhealed. Recent Barna Research across every age group, region , ethnicity , socio-economic status or faith segment indicates a staggering 84% believe there is significant anger and hostility between racial and ethnic groups in America. (Barna Trends, 2017). However, this hopeful statistic regarding "awareness" of the issue should NOT confuse or distract us from pursuing SOLUTIONS ! Jade's insights give solution-focused actions. As Jade rightly points out , a blanket "I'm sorry" or "Let's focus on what we have in common" ... hasn't worked and won't work. So what else can be done? .... Read this book and reap great rewards from Jade's sound counsel.

Gain abundantly from this great read as you are challenged to consider your own " comfort zones" . We all have a "comfort zone" where we sense adequacy , familiarity and "safety". Human nature seems wired to gravitate us toward where we feel adequate and to avoid the discomfort of our own inadequacies. Jade coveys a passionate hope for a maturity and faithfulness to ones's faith that demands we move beyond our "comfort zones" and courageously engage those "different" than us. Join Jade in this thoughtful journey with practical encouragements and you'll discover that we are all much more "alike than we are different" !

This book will move many out of the stands as spectators and into the game of extending love and forgiveness , understanding and compassion. May it be so.

Dr. David Ferguson, Co-Chair
Awakening America Alliance

"THIS FINELY WOVEN TAPESTRY GIVES ANSWERS"

"With a sensitivity born of experience and a passion for God's Word, which has the power to transform lives, Jade Lee addresses the deeper dimensions of an issue that has plagued our world since Genesis. Her diligent research not only informs but enlightens. Jade immediately draws her readers into this finely woven tapestry that gives biblical, historical, and practical answers for addressing the *Ferguson Dilemma* of prejudice and integrating cultures when emotions can bankrupt words. May each of us take seriously the challenge to not only bridge the gaps that divide us but see them eradicated in our generation."

—*Kay Horner, Executive Director*
Awakening America Alliance

"As the author of *The Ferguson Dilemma*, Jade has connected what occurred in Ferguson to the root of the issue in the Garden of Eden, rather than pointing to the single story of racism. James writes, *"My brethren do not hold the faith of our Lord Jesus Christ the Lord of glory, with partiality…if you fulfill the royal law according to Scripture, "you shall love your neighbor as yourself" you do well; but if you show partiality, you commit sin and are convicted by the law as a transgressor"* (James 2:1, 8-9, NKJV). How we, *"hold the faith of our Lord…"* is critical to our impact of culture as the body of Christ. Since the expansion of the His kingdom is directly connected to right relationships; we must get this right. Jade provides great insight into the essential relationship of loving God as the foundation of loving others well."

—Scott Gillum, Presiding Bishop
Texas Church of God of Prophecy
Pastor of Pastors, Houston, TX

"As a white-Anglo pastor, my heart is moved with godly sorrow to feel the historical and current pains of the black community in my reading of the *Ferguson Dilemma*. I recommend this book to every pastor seeking to see the power of the Gospel to bring miraculous racial reconciliation in today's hostile culture. From a growing friendship with Jade Lee, I appreciate how transparent and vulnerable she is in sharing this account and offering real solutions for healing."

—Dr. Michael S Lewis, Lead Pastor
Roswell Street Baptist Church, Marietta, GA

"My entire life has been given to the cause of racial unity. Over the years I have found that resources are key to equipping leaders and communities for the challenging work of healing racial wounds. The *Ferguson Dilemma* is a powerful tool bringing understanding, compassion, and a practical means for people of all backgrounds to feel adequate in engaging this vast subject. I highly recommend this book for all who desire to join the fight for racial redemption but don't know where to start. The *Ferguson Dilemma* is a great first step to lead your church, small groups, community organization or business toward a healed and unified America."

—Corey Lee, Pastor & Founder
Convergence Movement, Atlanta, GA

Acknowledgements

No man, or woman, is an island. It takes a village to raise a child. Because of the efforts of many personal, professional, and key thought leaders this book has been made possible. Many of the concepts in The Ferguson Dilemma reflect years of black history teaching, starting in a small New Jersey black Baptist church to the highly esteemed, Hampton University, English classes. I'll always be indebted to my parents, Neal and Robin Fisher, who instilled a love for culture in me, Hampton's professors who ensured all students knew their historical backdrop and the many Abolitionists, Civil Rights and Black history writers throughout time. Thank you for telling the untold stories that we need to heal.

To my personal assistant, Paige Smith, this book needed your wisdom and review to make that final touch exactly what was needed; your hours or selfless dedication to a cause you believed in are commendable. Thank you for being detail oriented, helping find the perfect resources and providing gentle but accurate feedback. You truly are a Spelman gem!

To my Convergence Church family, when we first planted this church we'd never known how many amazing people we would have met along the way. You have sacrificed hours of time so I could write this book for others. Thank you for valuing this call to writing. Your support means more than can be written in this short acknowledgement.

And last, but not least, to my husband and greatest cheerleader, Corey Lee, thank you for cooking meals, washing clothes, listening to hours of reading and encouraging me to keep writing, even when the end seemed impossible. Words cannot express my love and admiration of you. You are my greatest example of a servant's heart.

To My White Brothers and Sisters,

It has been a long, hard but rewarding road trying to find unity with one another. Our beginnings were not very great but the story of Redemption gives us all hope that we do not have to live in the past nor end our relationships the way they commenced.

Therefore, I want to offer you forgiveness, insight, encouragement and love. I want to challenge you to overcome the fear of white guilt, the past of your forefathers and having to carry the weight of your ancestor's decisions. We all have shameful details in our past that effect the next generations. May we learn the power of our decisions as we look back at history.

This book summaries black history from the colonization of Africa to the Civil Rights Movement in a chronological order and in laymen's terms. Hopefully it will reveal the undealt with injustices under our bridges of restoration.

Therefore, *The Ferguson Dilemma* is available to you, to help you hear the stories that have been buried due to fear. The reality is that there is an entire community still suffering because of these past mistreatments and you have the power of compassionate mourning in your hands. Your value is incomprehensible. You can be a generational pattern breaker with healing words and actions.

In fact, taking the time to know another perspective may be the first step to creating bridges with the most hardened, hurt people. Please do all that's in your power to reconcile. We need that in our day. Please do not remain silent when so many hurting people need to hear your voice on behalf of the white community.

May the William Lloyd Garrison's, who take the time to understand and act, arise in our day!

Blessings & Love.

Your Friend,

Jade Lee

To My Black Brothers and Sisters,

The title of Nelson Mandela's autobiography is true of us, it's been a *Long Walk to Freedom*. We cried, we sang, we prayed, we legislated and we marched but still our cry is oftentimes unheard. Our history has been buried, distorted, erased and neglected. We have been convinced that our story is less because it's black.

In an odd way, I find myself grateful for the current upheaval in our nation. It has awakened a sleeping giant to our greatness. Black students, who in 2006, laughed at slave stories, now mourn. They now embrace their curly locks, strong personalities and colorful history. It is an honor to be black in the Land of the Free, the Home of the Brave.

But we all know there is a lot more progress needed. We have been tempted to fall into utter disillusionment. *Maybe there is no way to ever advance? Maybe we will never be given equality. Will the powers that be continue to intentionally repackage injustice into another deceptive nightmare?*

My faith will not allow me to blame you, who have been through so much, forgiven those who mistreat you and live in current systematic challenges. Instead, it convicts me to Mourn with Those Who Mourn.

My faith will not allow me to be Hopeless either. You have risen through split family units, stripped of your identity, the grip of slavery, middle passage suicides, hundreds of hangings, empty promises, Jim Crow terrors and unavenged murders. You will continue to Arise, Be Better, Forgive, Love, Trust in the God that has brought you through. I challenge you to wear the cloak of love once more, to be the example your forefathers were to this great nation. But don't bow down to injustice.

Sing a song full of the faith that the dark past has taught us,
Sing a song full of the hope that the present has brought us;
Facing the rising sun of our new day begun,
Let us march on till victory is won.

Indebted to you,

Jade Lee

Introduction

I believe that unarmed truth and unconditional love will have the final word.
Dr. Martin Luther King Jr.

THE ART OF PREJUDICE

I am no stranger to prejudice. I am black. An expressive pastor's wife. A woman. American. Have a timeless baby face. And I have battled with infertility for 12 years.

All these factors come packaged with a set of preconceived notions: society's view of how I should act and what I should or should not know. These elements have quickly caused many people to talk down to me, get frustrated over my desire to express my age, thinking *"She must be in the youth group,"* believe me to be baby illiterate, and overlook me while greeting the pastor—my husband. These subtle encounters all revealed deeper messages of prejudice, often with underlying attacks on my personal knowledge, history or character.

Because most of these ideas are intricately woven into my core identity when the pain hits, it hits hard. But I would not trade the lessons I have learned from each of these experiences.

Presumptuous misconceptions have caused shock, pain, frustration, anger and even some fear. Shock that she really just said that. Pain that he did not take the time to get to know me. Frustration that they refuse to hear out truth. Anger that these injustices keep happening over and over without resolution. And fear that the cycle may never be broken.

For example, any given Sunday night, during our worship experience I may receive a scowling look of disapproval, a cold shoulder from someone I tried to embrace, a stone frozen look from the person with deeply set offenses. I may be greeted with a "lesson" from the visitor assuming I don't know what I'm doing and need a talking to…At first this was shocking to see that common courtesy often left people when they found themselves interacting with a pastor's wife.

You may be absolutely ignored as a visitor greets your husband standing beside you then as they begin to vent their most recent catastrophe. You chime in to make them aware that you are standing right there and do exist.

You smile as bright and happy as you know how. The person you are greeting looks back at you with a scowl. You thought the unspoken rule was, 'I smile at you, you smile back.' Unfortunately, this is not always the case when dealing with a pastor's wife. The knowledge that she must forgive, can be taken advantage of even innocently by people.

You say hello to the mother or grandmother exiting your service, attempting to share another basic yet welcoming greeting. They begin to school you on how to take care of children as they have judged that clearly you do not know. The assumptions begin. You do not have kids and must not have ever cared for a child, taught a children's class nor looked at TLC. You are clueless to the fact that two year olds have fits and babies cry throughout the night. Their thoughts are clear. There is no way you could know anything about that as a childless woman.

You nod your head and smile because this is what is expected of you, clearly.

Never respond back, be too frank or speak too much. Stand, be beautiful, and smile as much as you can.

And when you go to mentor, pray for or enter the world of a newly pregnant mommy you get another talking to about all that you clearly must not know about pregnancy.

Yet what is not considered is that you do have an opinion and valuable experience. You have studied the Bible yourself. God gave you a voice. You love children and used to teach every age from infancy to kindergarten. You mentored single moms and helped raise their children day to day. Repeatedly, you have played the doula role, sitting in the joy of watching a newborn's arrival.

What is not considered is that you have been taking traumatized children from the age of 0-18 for the past 8 years into your home, "mothering" them back to a state of peace, self-control, and dignity. You have been helping 18-35 year olds find their way in life- getting calls from their teachers when they don't perform well in college, teaching them how to read and write on a college level, mentoring them through life-skills, and watching them move on into marriage, parenting and the real world.

When you finally, that one time, speak up for yourself, you are condemned to being a mean, controlling unwelcoming woman. All because you did not fit into other's prejudgments of how a first lady should perform.

Inside. You feel like you are 50. Outside. You look like you are 23. Inside you know you have mothered countless. Outside. Others simply see you have never physically birthed a child. Not many will understand.

This is the art of prejudice.

THE ART OF RACISM

A few years ago, a television series came out about being Black in America. It was a wonderful depiction of what it may be like to be black and the issues African Americans face daily. [Of course, if you are black, it is easy to relate to almost all the accounts in that series. Being black in America is a rich, cultural, historic journey, but there are deeply rooted perspectives you must constantly confront.]

Oftentimes people are not even aware they have believed falsehoods about who you are; nevertheless, beliefs—especially those based on false assumptions—can be very harmful to our society and to one another.

Just as many people find it hard to understand my experiences as a Black-Christian-woman in her early thirties playing a "mother" placebo role…people don't always get what it is like to be black in America.

Many come into encounters with black people the same way,

sizing them up, making a judgment on how old they are, how educated, how successful and their economic status. *Maybe this black guy is a thief or a thug. Maybe this girl is promiscuous like the girls in the hip hop music videos.*

Racism- Belief or doctrine asserting racial differences in character, intelligence, etc. and the superiority of one race over another or others: racist doctrine, also, typically, seeks to maintain the supposed purity of a race or the races.

Webster's New World College Dictionary

Elism- A prejudgment of the nature of GOD beyond factual evidence.

Defined for The Ferguson Dilemma

Prejudice- Preconceived judgment or opinion, an adverse opinion or learning formed without just grounds or before sufficient knowledge

Merriam Webster's Dictionary

Or *maybe they are all incredibly dangerous angry people when you get on their bad sides?*

These underlining views did not come out of thin air. They came from whispered household conversations, spoken visualizations of who people of African descent are…they came from dark places of thought and expression.

Yet nothing is new under the sun.

And people have had these conversations for a very long time. (In fact, the first two people had a conversation leading to a judgmental mentality, and consequential relational division.) It all started with a twisted discussion behind someone else's back.

That gossipy beginning caused the perfect world of the Garden of Eden to be disrupted. And what happened in Adam and Eve's hearts is too relevant in solving our current racial dilemma to ignore. For the sake of clear communication, in this book, we will refer to The Garden of Eden prejudice as **Elism- A prejudgment of the nature of God beyond factual evidence.**

THE FIRST PREJUDICED CONVERSATION

From the beginning of time, GOD established The Family Unit. He longed for both man and woman, Adam and Eve, to enjoy one another. He created a beautiful world, a garden full of pleasurable experiences for them to grow their family:

GOD blessed them and said to them, "Be fruitful and increase in number; fill the earth and subdue it. Rule over the fish in the sea and the birds in the sky and over every living creature that moves on the ground."

GOD had amazing plans set out for Adam and Eve- there was no need for retirement. Adam and Eve didn't struggle with family-work-life balance. They didn't wonder how they would get it all done. Everything was at their fingertips and all was well. Then the unthinkable occurred.

In the book, *Unashamed,* there is a fitting excerpt on the downfall that broke Adam and Eve's delightful reality. This explanation is helpful in visualizing the first instance of prejudice:

> "In the very beginning of everything GOD began to create a place for Adam and Eve to exist and enjoy. He was making a home for His children and He was the very first "happily ever after" novelist. As He was creating, He was also solving a major problem: A Lack of Form, Emptiness and Darkness. This is the extent He went to before even making humanity; He wanted to ensure that all was well. They were not born into a messy, empty, dark world. He was preparing a place for them as His Son would do for us thousands of years later (see John 14:2).

But after all was well, GOD *saw.* Remember, when GOD saw this was a look of *approval* and blessing.[1] Until this point all is *good*, but something in Eve's perspective of GOD's creation and heart towards her Creator began to shift.

The word *ra'ah* is used to describe the instance Eve "saw" the tree of the knowledge of good and evil in a different light. GOD spoke to Adam about the Tree of the Knowledge of Good and Evil before Eve was created. He told Adam not to eat of it or he would die. Although Eve knew GOD's desire concerning this tree, she found herself standing right next to it- facing temptation. We all know seeing others as less is wrong but we stand face-to-face with

---

[1] Strongs #7200. The New Strong's Concordance

Introduction

America's tree of temptation- Racism.

In our household conversations, secret thoughts and quiet fears we can relate to this first judgmental experience:

> [1]Now the serpent was more crafty than any of the wild animals the LORD God had made. He said the woman, "Did God really say, 'You must not eat from any tree in the garden'?" [2]The woman said to the serpent, "We may eat fruit from the trees in the garden, [3]but God did say, 'You must not eat fruit from the tree that is in the middle of the garden, and you must not touch it, or you will die.'" (Genesis 3:1-3, KJV).

Either Eve did not hear GOD's message correctly when Adam translated what GOD told him or she was adding extra instructions to GOD's command- probably the latter considering that Adam was perfect. He had no memory issues at this point in time. GOD's original instruction to Adam is provided in Genesis 2:16-17:

> [16]And the LORD God commanded the man, "You are free to eat from any tree in the garden; [17]but you must not eat from the tree of the knowledge of good and evil, for when you eat from it you will certainly die."

It is evident in GOD's instruction He did not want Adam and Eve to eat from the tree of the knowledge of good and evil. However, GOD never told them they could not *touch* it; Eve's perspective was beginning to be influenced by the serpent's *subtle influence*. The serpent was on a mission to present GOD as harsh and demanding. He wanted Eve to begin thinking she was missing out on true life, she was being mistreated. The serpent began this convincing, asking Eve if she could eat of every tree of the garden. At this point, we can presume what Eve's mind may have been pondering, *Why didn't GOD allow me to eat of every tree? Was He trying to keep something from me? Is GOD as good as He says He is?* She is clearly negatively influenced by the time she mentions not being able to touch the tree of the knowledge of good and evil, something God had never Himself said.

The plot thickens. Now that the serpent has lured Eve in, he tells a bold-face lie: *Ye shall not surely die…*This was in direct conflict with GOD's previous message: thou shalt not eat of it: for in the day that thou eatest thereof thou shalt surely die (Genesis 2:17). Eve had to choose whether she would believe GOD or the serpent. Because of her internal-desire for the fruit, she chose the serpent. He continued to connive Eve with more accusations saying, "For GOD doth know that in the day ye eat thereof, then your eyes shall be opened, and ye shall be as gods, knowing good and evil." (Genesis 3:5, KJV).

BLURRY VISION

Racism, like Elism, stops us from seeing clearly. Our eyesight blurs out reality. When we begin with preconceived notions, it is very hard to give new experiences a clean slate. Adam and Eve judged GOD based on what the serpent stated rather than their own experiences.

After this mental tug-of-war Eve is pulled completely to the enemy's side. She then sees differently.

This prejudice or elism, against GOD brought shame received from this first racist act causing Adam and Eve to delve deeper into sin. They began playing the blame game, inaccurately judging others and prematurely listening to other's opinions.

We continue to live out these traits today.

We have judged one another due to who we believe the other is and how we believe they should behave. We then blame them when they create their own historical narrative or voice. It is hard to let go of our old viewpoints to acknowledge when we have been wrong.

As a nation, we are now faced with the challenges of overcoming the underlining issue of Racism, but we do not always know how to change our views. Time and time again, it can seem as though racism is beginning to lose its hold, only for its unwelcomed grip to rise back into newspaper headlines, mirroring our darkened history.

We march, we protest, we cry out, we apologize, we forgive, but it never seems to *fully subside*. From generation to generation, racism resurfaces making it undeniable: **We have yet to Deal with its One Root—the spiritual sickness plaguing the soul of our great nation.** Racism is not a tangible object, but its effects are quite substantial. Although it starts with a thought that "cannot be touched," one thought can soon become an underlining "doctrine" in the mind of the racist.[2] If acted upon it can appear in the way of a negative comment, slur or action. These actions can be as seemingly innocent as watching someone suspiciously in a store and as

---

[2] Webster's Dictionary (intangible and racism)

devastating as gunning someone down due to their skin complexion.

Likewise, experiences such as isolation or mistreatment due to one's skin color can be very harmful because just as I cannot change the fact that I am a woman, black or look young, colorism is intrinsically related to identity. The scary reality is this sort of prejudice is easily denied by the other race. Like a cancer, it is unseen to the naked eye. Because American society tends to see the material prior to seeing the immaterial, racial prejudice strongly affects one's psyche.

Figure 1 The Race Cycle

Experience ⟩ Seed Thought ⟩ Belief ⟩ Doctrine ⟩ Racism ⟩ Racist Action

1965

Watts Riots, Los Angeles

2014-2015

Ferguson, MO

For example, the common saying, "Sticks and stones can break my bones but words can never hurt me," although seemingly true, could not be further from the truth. Both words and thoughts can have drastic effects on the human soul.

In talking to a sample of African American, African and Caribbean youth between the ages of 19 and 25, they shared some racist experiences in their own lives, revealing that prejudice words, thoughts and actions can have long term effects:[3]

> "…when I was younger I was constantly followed around stores when I walked in especially with other people. If I was with people of other races they wouldn't follow them, just me or the other black people I was with…" (20-ish African American woman)

> "…in 8th grade when I moved to Georgia. I was walking to my friends house and these group of white guys in a car screamed unidentifiable slurs and (threw) trash at me while they drove by."

STICKS & STONES

"Sticks and stones may break my bones but words will never hurt me." This popular saying couldn't be further from the truth. Can you think of a time another's words and thoughts have affected you? Maybe as a child or even as an adult those words seem to follow you. The same goes for racial slurs and thoughts.

---

[3] Some of these quotes may have been edited for clarity purposes but the meaning of the quote has not been tampered.

"In 11th grade when I moved back to Georgia after leaving for a year I experienced racism at school. When I transferred to a new school the advisor put me in a remedial math class, which pushed me back and made me have to earn more math credits. The previous year at the school before I got a B in math. And she kept telling me about how I wouldn't be able to make it to a four-year college, she misguided me on my schedule, which eventually caused me to have to take a full load my senior year with advance math classes, two sciences, advanced Spanish classes and English." (19 year old African American male)

These statements bring clarity on what racism could look like in our current times. Oftentimes in defining racism it is easy to say, "*I am not behaving or thinking that way. I can assure you, I'm not racist.*" But when seen from the other parties' perspective our actions could be very harmful. **Both overt and covert racism** are present in the above stories.

UNSEEN PAINS

Oxford Dictionary defines Covert as "not openly acknowledged or displayed" and Overt as "done or shown openly; plainly apparent." Racism whether shrewdly hidden in a school system or openly declared in a playground causes Unseen Pains, exposing Hidden Prejudice.

If indeed the young man's advisor made a suggestion that he not even try applying to a four-year college, out of a racist mentality about African American boys in that moment, covert racism was occurring. This is not the only story amongst African Americans of its sort. The reasoning behind following the group of black youth in a store could very well be racism.

Time and time again, it can seem as though racism is beginning to lose its hold, only for its unwelcomed grip to rise back into newspaper headlines, mirroring our darkened history.

Other instances of racism are more overt, although both open and hidden racial acts are direct attacks against a victimized person.

The example of the boy walking with his friends as a group of young white boys screamed racial slurs at them was very overt. Examples of black youth being marginalized abound in the United States of America, yet there remains an ongoing argument on whether the discussion of racism is relevant in modern times.

Oftentimes, it is not overt forms of racism that are most hurtful; it is covert, harder to prove acts that produce a deeper pain. Although difficult, covert acts may be more unexpected because they are oftentimes shrewdly hidden in acts of omission or insinuation such as not being invited to a party because of one's skin complexion or talked behind one's back then treated kindly in person. This may cause a greater shock and recovery effect.

Examples of black youth being marginalized abound in the Unites States of America, yet there remains an ongoing argument on whether the discussion of racism is relevant in modern times.

Racism is not just a socially taboo act that is hurtful to others; it is in direct violation to GOD. When we don't joyfully accept GOD's creation, we are not accepting Him.

Imagine being a parent and someone verbally or physically abuses your child due to who they are- too short, too tall, too outspoken, too quiet. An involved and caring parent would be bothered by this injustice and feel like not only was his child mistreated, but it was a direct wrongdoing to them as a legal guardian.

Likewise, when we are not willing to fully accept and love others because they are different than what we are used to, we are directly hurting the heart of GOD.

Introduction

Jesus said it like this, Truly I tell you, whatever you did for one of the least of these brothers and sisters of mine, you did for me...For I was hungry and you gave me nothing to eat, I was thirsty and you gave me nothing to drink." [4]

This Scripture reveals Jesus' perspective on how we treat others. When we aim to restore relationship by uprooting racist thoughts we are doing one of the most powerful and spiritual acts of love we could for the children of God.

The good news is that no matter how many times I am told I look like a baby, or am talked down to, or ignored, God teaches me new lessons in each painful moment. Others have come back over and over again to apologize once realizing they made a judgment that was not based on truth.

The black community has been through this sort of experience repeatedly and throughout generations. The white community is continuing to learn how to relate to a people that have lived IN biased situations for many years.

But the battle is not hopeless.

The more we listen for truth and are willing to let go of old thought patterns, we will begin to bridge the gaps that have caused ongoing misunderstanding. There is hope for a New Beginning. If we remain committed to this process, together, **We Shall Overcome.**

---

[4] Matthew 25:40, 42 (NIV)

Chapter 1
Racial Roots

"Racism springs from the lie that certain human beings are less than fully human. It's a self-centered falsehood that corrupts our minds into believing we are right to treat others as we would not want to be treated."
Alveda King

BLIND SPOTS

It's funny how our discontentment can lead to self-discovery. For years I did not understand my husband's sweet gentle spirit. I took it for granted and even for a weakness. I wanted to see strength. Now, before you judge me or misunderstand, I deeply value my husband and appreciate who he is, but just could not wrap my mind around this aspect of his personality. It was foreign to me.

I wanted to see strength. And boy was my image of strength skewed! This man was gentle, loving and submitted to God. He was not controlling nor demanding. Instead, he exuded a great measure of self-control.

To me, *if I was honest with myself,* this was not how I believed a man should carry himself. He should demand respect, be overly protective and keep others in their place when they wronged him.

He should be "strong."

It took me years to come to terms or really even see how skewed my perspective was, but eventually God healed my sight. One morning, as I sat with my husband, who daily ministered to me through the Word, it dawned on me that he was so similar to the docile yet competent personality of Dr. King in the area of, not passiveness, but gentleness. I was so blessed to be able to give him one of the greatest compliments I could give, "You remind me of Dr. King."

As these words surprisingly slipped out of my mouth his interest was peaked, "How so?" he asked inquisitively. I began to share many ways Dr. King turned the other cheek and the words of my father came to mind, "Corey, you are a man of peace."

This is when it dawned on me that I do not need a man of war or heavily demonstrated fierceness. *There are times when the greatest measure of manhood is found in the quiet strength of a man who has learned to get out of the way and allow God to fight his battles.*

As all of this began to hit me, I realized the relational problem was never him, it was me. It was my perspective of how to get my need for protection met. And it was my flawed view of what a man who protected me should look like. There was nothing wrong with wanting my husband to stand up for me or "put people in their place" in defending our family. But I had to learn to embrace his way of doing it through prayer and love. I had to learn that maybe the issue was my all or nothing mentality.

ARE WE FACING "THE ROOT"?

The same goes for finding "the root" to our racial divisiveness. Whether we like it or not we have been "married" to one another, we live in the same home. For the sake of national peace, we must figure out how to make this work. But have we spent too much time on symptoms, never getting to the heart of what is wrong?

The root of racism may extend further back than we think; it can arguably be found in the first breech of humanity, but it is not with two opposing races. Instead, it is found in the heart of a woman and her mindset about her GOD. The root can therefore be established as a **deceptive sway of the heart in regards to her mentality about who GOD is and how GOD feels about her (intention-wise).**

This lie then bred discontentment with perfection. In fact, it was in a state of perfect bliss that the first human altercation occurred. This altercation stemmed from man stepping outside GOD's Safety Boundaries. Distrust and disobedience caused mankind to become at aught with one another. Before this moment, all was well and there was not a need for any level of contention.

Imagine a place where there was no division, conflict, contention or argumentation. Adam and Eve were in perfect unity with both GOD and one another. Since then, we all desperately long for this place. As we see war, hunger, racism, and injustice prevail the desire increases. We want wrong to become right, but we do not know exactly how to right apparent wrongs. This is where we begin to come into serious conflict- the How question is an essential barrier to cross if we ever want to get beyond only acknowledging the race-problems in our world.

For the past 12 years I have been studying and living in the black community, searching for answers to our crisis. I went to a historically black university, was raised in both a lower income and middle class community, and have chosen to live in the second highest crime rate neighborhood of Atlanta. To say the least, this burden for my people group has been ingrained and developed within me over time.

There are times when the greatest measure of manhood is found in the quiet strength of a man who has learned to get out of the way and allow God to fight his battles.

Throughout these years I have been in various discussions about the issues in the black community, stemming back to slavery, and how to properly address these issues. But the honest truth is, the majority of these conversations never really focused on true change or progression. Many of them simply highlighted, re-highlighted and then shifted around the problems. Lots of pain, most of it very warranted, can be heard as we discuss these issues in detail, discover our history and wonder how to heal the black community. How do we heal these racial issues once and for all?

Is it through continuing to try the racial reconciliation route?

Changing the mindset of the white community? Becoming a middle class citizen and achieving social change? Changing government and policy? Moving to the inner city, where the problems are most glaringly evident? Beginning to raise the next generation through the family unity? Or simply saying that it's all over...it's time to move on?

In all of my studies, conversations and observations there is a pretty clear conclusion: this issue goes deeper than the color of one's skin or a community plan, although acknowleding both are needed to produce results. This issue cannot be dealt with on a root level without going back to the real source- **Sin**.

Let's revisit the garden. Remember, the idea of pitting one person or people group against another with a hidden agenda (the desire to reign in dominion) is nothing new:

Now the serpent was more cunning than any beast of the field which the LORD GOD had made. (Genesis 3:1, NKJV)

After being shifted out of his comfort zone, sent down to utter darkness, the serpent appears in the garden, trying to regain dominion. He was not going to just deceive Adam and Eve into believing his questioning against GOD's intentions. And he could not get dominion from God, but he could convince the people God gave dominion to transfer it over to him. He began to lure them into his lies. He caused them to question GOD's heart by asking them questions. As they began to ponder these questions, they soon turned away from their former allegiance to GOD, hiding from their Creator and leaning on the words of the serpent.

LIES AND MISCONCEPTIONS

This is exactly how racism works. It's all the idea that you cannot trust another race because of your differences (which happen to be the color of your skin). These differences are all the reason to begin to look down on another race. Before you know it you are caught up in this battle between one another. You are questioning the other race. You can no longer see what is common between the two of you.

It's the same marital problem I was having with my husband. Sin and deception, a push of the enemy caused me to place blame on Corey. *It's his fault. He should change. His personality is not enough.* But, in reality, it was my inability to see my flaws. It was my inability to see how much I was being pushed to question his integrity or how God created him.

Upon questioning GOD's words, which represent His integrity, Eve made the same relational faux pas. She gradually turned from GOD. *Maybe he is tricking me, maybe He's not for me, He's got another agenda or plan in mind that I don't know of…so I have to protect myself.* Once these questions begin to settle in, we find ourselves in a mess. Before long, Eve was having an entire conversation with the serpent about what GOD said. This conversation was deeper than the words GOD said, it was about GOD's heart.

Eve fell for the lie about His integrity, feeling like she was missing out on something, *"…but of the fruit of the tree which is in the midst of the garden, GOD has said, 'You shall not eat it, nor shall you touch it, lest you die."*[5] The problem with her reasoning was that deception

---

5
Genesis 3:3, NJKV

is only partial truth. She knew GOD gave her an instruction not to eat of the tree, but He never told her not to touch it.

She was deceived into believing that GOD was worse than what He really was…he was trying to control her and take something away from her. But GOD was only trying to protect her. She was now being pit against GOD, all based on a misunderstanding, something she heard about Him that was not really true.

Before long, Eve was having an entire conversation with the serpent about what God said. This conversation was deeper than the words God said, it was about God's heart.

In racism, the misconception about another people group may be based off of some truth or fact- it may have to do with the color of their skin, the size of their nose, the part of town they are from, or the loudness of their conversation. But when this fact is clouded with a negative tone, racism begins to form in the heart of the viewer. It is then that a superior attitude forms in that person's heart.

This can begin with a simple conversation you hear about another people group as a child. Or it can happen as an isolated incident, a rare encounter with another race, affects you negatively. This incident or conversation may have nothing to do with an entire people group, but it has you stunned. In response, you must gather reasoning for this person's behavior or the information you heard about this individual. You have a choice to dig deeper, seek out the truth or assume that what you experienced is accurate concerning an entire people group. In other words, the commonality for you becomes the color of the person's skin as opposed to the content of the person's character.

Similarly, when Eve was in the Garden of Eden, she began to get caught up in the words GOD said, forgetting to examine the true character or heart of GOD. *What was her personal experience with GOD?* She came to the conclusion that what she was overhearing was true, but it was intentional manipulation to cause Eve to fall out of unity with the one who loved her most. At that point the serpent was able to connive her into

UNPROVEN NOTIONS

The point we believe that a person's character, on a heart level, is off due to a presented but unproven notion is the point we develop a prejudice. Many prejudices about the black community have formed causing a leaning toward the notion that their situation is their fault and they should be more responsible without consideration of their background pre and during slavery.

believing GOD was lying to her about dying when she ate of the fruit. She was now developing a prejudice regarding GOD based off of a complete inaccuracy.

GOD was being misrepresented and Satan had won his goal to create division. Hence, you have the idea of Dividing and Conquering with a political agenda to win a nation of people. The root of Satan's agenda was greed. He wanted to win the heart of Adam and Eve so he could have control over their actions, hence the world. He wanted to win this battle over GOD and he knew the best way to do it was by winning the heart of the people GOD created.

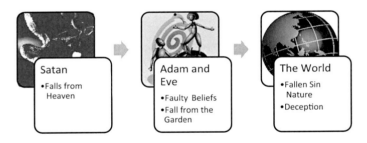

This sort of phenomenon still occurs politically today and occurred in nations before us, as we will discover throughout this book. Greed caused the devastating levels of slavery we have seen throughout history. And because of Greed, the enemy did not want Adam and Eve to continue to rule the earth. Unfortunately, the conclusion of Eve's story is a great fall. She shares the fruit with Adam, who was with her throughout the entire conversation. He eats the fruit and they fall into sin together.

Deep inside, Adam and Eve knew they were wrong to judge GOD without giving Him a fair chance to speak for Himself. They began to hide behind fear and blame, revealing how their decision literally divided their own hearts. When we are divided from GOD it is impossible to be fully united with one another.

Sin inherently separates man from GOD and man from man. Sin causes us to look at the other party, failing to see what we have done wrong or could have done better in the situation. Racism is a form of this issue. We can find ourselves blaming another race for our own issues.

When we realize that we are no longer simply a victim, we become a victor. There is a power in taking responsibility. It enables us to move on from devastating situations.

The reality is that true help comes by self-evaluation and acceptance for our own shortcomings. It is then and only then that we reach out for help, feeling true sorrow for our actions. The Bible refers to this as Godly Sorrow. There were serious consequences for Adam and Eve's actions, which all began with a concept. And there are serious consequences for racism as well, which all begins with a concept…a simple thought about another human being or people group.

This is where we really need *Aha Moments*. These are the moments that we begin to have Thought Shifting Epiphanies. It is like the moment that I realized, the problem is not my husband, it is my perception of him. And, when I shift, the problem will be solved.

NEXT GEN PROBLEMS

This is the power of the thought. What we think determines how we will behave and treat others within our influence. After sinful thoughts in the Garden, life continued, but more sin grew. In the following generation, Cain's viewpoint of his brother matured into murder. This was due to Cain coveting his brother, Abel's blessing… When he couldn't get it, he took Cain's life.

When GOD questioned Cain's actions, mirroring his parents questioning in the Garden, Cain responded with an attitude, "Am I my brother's keeper?" GOD made it clear to Cain that there was a right and wrong way to receive the same blessing, *"Why are you angry? And why has your countenance fallen? If you do well, will you not be accepted? And if you do not do well, sin lies at the door. And its desire is for you, but you should rule over it."*[6]

Cain wanted the results of his brother's obedience without the sacrifice required for him to obtain a similar outcome. Because

---

BELIEVING A LIE

Deep inside, Adam and Eve knew they were wrong to judge God without giving Him a fair chance to speak for Himself. We have done the same to one another for centuries. There are times that we listen to the accuser, who may be a friend who is "venting," a loved one who has an issue with another person or race, or an enemy who appears as a buddy. No matter how these seeds of distrust are planted into our hearts about others, it is so important that we begin to guard our ears from words of accusation. We want to ask God to guide and lead us to truth.

6
Genesis 4:6-7, NIV

of Cain's attitude, he became the world's first murderer. This deep hatred evolved in only one generation after Adam and Eve's fall. It was now clear that GOD had Adam and Eve's best interest in mind. This had to break their hearts as parents. There was no previous situation preparing their minds for the trauma of fratricide. The impact of this is unimaginable.

Through the loss of a son at a sibling's hands, one could see the deep, fatherly love of GOD in warning them about not eating of the

The truth always has a way of coming out after the consequences to the lies we believe become self evident. Life has a way of guiding us pass the blindspots of our hearts.

---

tree in the Garden. He wanted them to reign in dominion and live a happy, prosperous life, but sin hindered this from occurring. Sin has heartbreaking results. The corruption that is capable in the human heart is deeply tied to breaking the law of GOD.

As descendants of Adam and Eve, we all now need His grace to overcome such a deeply engraved issue. This is why we need the Gospel to overcome our tendency towards selfishness and self-promotion:

For all have sinned and fall short of the glory of GOD, being justified freely by His grace through the redemption that is in Christ Jesus, whom GOD set forth as a propitiation by His blood, through faith, to demonstrate His righteousness, because in His forbearance GOD had passed over the sins that were previously committed, to demonstrate at the present time His righteousness, that he might be just and the justifier of the one who has faith in Jesus. (Romans 3:23-26, NKJV)

GOD's answer to a broken, divided people has been and will always be a Mediator. He has a bridge, a lawyer, that will bring the two parties back to the truth. This person will first bring them back to GOD and then GOD will bring them to the place of reconciliation. As we both see our wrong concepts, judgments and prejudices, healing begins. Then we come back to GOD, apologizing for how we have viewed His creation. We ask for His perspective of the other party, which is many times different than our own. We humble ourselves as we see the greatest mediator of all, Jesus Christ, step in to heal both of our broken hearts.

It is then and only then that we fall in love with the person we deemed our polar enemy. We want to love them because we are in love with the Man who loved them first. He loved us all in the midst of personal need and now we want to extend that same forgiveness to others.

Racism exposes a great need. It not only hurts the victim, but the racist needs help as well. The racist has been deceived to attack his brother and will suffer dire consequences due to the principle of sowing and reaping. Racism is a sickness of the human heart which must be addressed on a heart (spiritual) level if it is ever to be uprooted. This is why America has seen its days of freedom from physical slavery and civil slavery, but has yet to see its need for freedom from this spiritual bondage: the enslavement of the heart. Once this revelation is obtained, a great awakening of deep love will begin.

A revival of relationships will begin in the home, in the community, in the church and in the marketplace. This is what the soul of a broken nation is deeply longing for, but it will not occur through Cain's mentality of taking needs. We must all begin the work of introspection, acknowledging our own needs, asking GOD to come into our own heart so we can love as He loves. This unconditional love will break the chains unknowingly remaining in our hearts. It will tear down barriers that seemed impossible a moment before, enabling us to overcome years of deeply rooted hurt and pain.

REFLECTION QUESTIONS

1. Have you ever developed a perspective of someone else based a secondhand comment about that person or an isolated experience, only to find that it was not true?

2. What did you learn about not judging situations or people too quickly?

3. How can this prepare you to see others as God sees them, not based on popular opinion or accusations?

4. In reading this chapter, what have you learned about how our human hearts can have blind spots?

5. David prayed the prayer, "LORD, try the reigns of my heart and see if there be any wicked way in me." Pray this prayer asking GOD to reveal any hidden racial viewpoints you have against another race. Journal what He showed you.

Chapter 2
Colonization Aftermaths

"the most…tragic – of these changes took place …from 1890 and 1910,
the period that saw the conquest and occupation of virtually
the whole continent of Africa by the imperial powers
and the establishment of the colonial system."
A. Adu Boahen

WHY UNDERSTAND THE ROOT

I can remember sitting in my high school classroom, dumbfounded by both my teacher and my textbook.

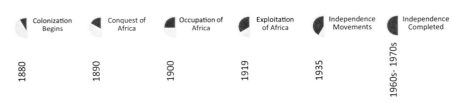

Figure 3 From Colonization to Independence, 1880-1970s

Why was there only one and a half pages on the colonization of Africa, slavery, emancipation, The Middle Passage and The Civil Rights Movement? But we spent our entire 6th grade year discussing the injustices of Germany's Jewish holocaust. Why did my teacher nervously fumble around with his hands, while avoiding all contact with the black students in the class? He was trying to move on from this topic as quick as humanly possible. But we, as the black community in the class, although few, were not squeamish about talking through our rich history. It was a part of who we were as individuals. We were tired of being ignored and dismissed.

The danger of this type of mis- to -absent education in regards to America's racial history is clear-cut in our modern racial war. When we do not have this background constant arguments over why blacks are still upset, misunderstandings and blanket ignorance occur. This is now a Real Dilemma. It is time for both blacks and whites to learn what colonization really was like for both parties involved, to connect the dots to our current issues. This chapter will provide you with a brief view of the historical facts oftentimes missed or misconstrued in our education system.

As a direct result to the discovery of Africa is often being disregarded in American classrooms, questions frequently arise such as, Who discovered who? What did they find? From who's perspective is the story of colonization typically told? Have we adequately explored the African perspective of this story line or have Africans been permanently etched in our minds as those "found" by the heroic colonizer? Were Africans ever really lost or in "need" of help to develop their "barbaic" land? What was the relationship between African leaders and Europeans prior to colonization?

Understanding the facts behind false portrayals of pre-colonized Africa, can reestablish generational concepts that trickle down, unknowingly causing us to adopt mentalities that shape how we view black descendants.

Colonialism
Control by one country over another area and its people.
(Merriam-Webster)

As these perspectives accrue there is typically an overflow into one's behaviors whether stemming from a conscious or a subconscious level. As we begin to look at these historical events from both sides of the color line, like a mirror reflecting history, we see more accurately the world, our nation, our communities, our families and ourselves. As we see ourselves we change. As we see others more accurately, our view changes as well and the faulty perceptions causing racism are bound to subside.

Africans were taken into "colonialism" by force, against their will, making the term "colonialism itself a type of euphemism for enforced servanthood. We are all familiar with the danger of wanting control that is not given to us.

We have to be careful not to operate in a domineering spirit. We must be careful to relinquish our need for control and desire to have more than what has been given to us by GOD. We must not use our power to take what belongs to others without their consent. Colonization was the rape of an entire continent, people group and thousands of individuals, by a people we have oftentimes considered "heroes," but Africans would have seen as inhumanely oppressive. Colonization was the rape of an entire continent, people group and thousands of individuals, by a people we have oftentimes considered "heroes," but Africans would have seen as inhumanely oppressive.

This is why people of African descent, especially the displaced, are a lost people without Jesus. I am mostly interested in conveying the personal and spiritual effect that colonialism had on an entire people group. I want to convey to white people how deep this goes and how terrible it felt for the African race.

I want to establish understanding of the heart of black people so others can begin to relate to the commonality of the human race: Pain. I do this

RACISM, TODAY?

When we go to the doctor and realize we have a virus it's usually due to unwelcomed symptoms. Today we see symptoms of a relational problem throughout our society but sometimes we do not want to face the fact that racism may be a virus we need healing from. What are signs that this may still be at play in our culture or in our subconscious?

in hopes to reconcile relationship through deep repentance without defense, the type of repentance that simply states, "I was wrong." But I also want to convey how Caucasians were generationally effected in negative ways by the colonization and eventual enslavement of Africans. Even the oppressor is traumatized by the injustices they cause. It is a painful experience to revisit the history of a supremacist ancestral line.

Africans were taken into "colonialism"
by force, against their will, making
the term "colonialism" a type of
euphemism for enforced servanthood.

For Europeans, this period of time is considered 'colonialism' but for the Africans this is a period of 'the strategy of resistance of protest in Africa'; (Boahen 14). *History written from a white person's perspective is very different than history written from an African's perspective.*

As humans, on an individual and corporate level, we tend to fail in seeing the other's perspective.

We are mainly focused on our own gain. It is not until devastation takes over our peace that we are many times forced into action, realizing the gravity of our selfish mistakes. Akin to how history has been written from a biased perspective, it must be revisited if we want to find truth. Time must be taken to hear both the black and white perspective of colonization and slavery.

Even the oppressor is traumatized by
the injustices they cause. It is a painful experience
to revisit the history of a supremacist ancestral line.

What did Africans feel when their nations were suddenly taken by Europeans? This was more than an institution, government or organization. This was people, families and hearts broken as they watched life as they always knew it stripped before their eyes.

The reality? There were already established cultures and various African people groups that were misunderstood and devalued, deemed as less, by Europeans. These were a people with dignity, political order, kings and queens. And prior to colonization, they were accustomed to interacting with European culture.

THE BEGINNINGS OF RACISM

African Racism did not begin with the grand scale European break in; it initiated with deeply rooted "racist legends" well before the official Slave Trade and Middle Passage commencement. Due to these tales, the mentalities that drive slavery were already ingrained into European culture. These are the same views that have been passed down hundreds of years later in the United States of America.

Until the lions have their own
historians, the history of the hunt
will always glorify the hunter.

Chinua Achebe

Digging through the murky pile of racist history, we find a rare diamond, a light-filled prism dividing truth. The following 16th century narrative would be a great oversight to disregard in our discussion on colonization. In 1156, Pliny's first century, *Summary of the Antiquities and Wonders of the World* was published. Take note of the description of African Ethiopians here:

Of the Ethiopians there are divers forms and kinds of men.

Some there are toward the east that have neither nose nor nostrils, **but the face all full.** Others that have no upper lip, they are without tongues, and they speak by signs, and they have but a little hole to take their breath at, by the which they drink with an oaten straw. There are some called Syrbote that are eight feet high, **they live with the chase of elephants.** In a part of Affricke be people called Ptoemphane, for their king they have a dog,

One cannot understand the heart of modern blacks until one knows their historical storyline.

at whose fancy they are governed...Toward the west there is a people called Arimaspi, that have but one eye in their foreheads, **they are in the desert and wild country.** The people called Agriphagi **live with the flesh of panthers and lions:** and the people called Anthropomphagi **which we call cannibals,** live with human flesh. The Cinamolgi, their heads are almost like to the heads of dogs...Others called Gramantes, **they make no**

marriages, but all women are common. Gamphasantes **they go all naked.** Blemmyis a people so called, they have no heads, but have their mouth and their eyes in their breasts. And others there are that go [**walk**] **more by training of their hands than with their feet** (Reader 325-326, bold added).

This passage, revealing a potential root of slavery, was resurrected in 1556. This resurgence of racist propaganda has been occurring for centuries, but this time it was about to birth the international trade of human cargo. When scholars write about topics in a biased, prejudiced manner we are faced with a generational thought pattern that passes to their descendants in various forms. Over time, when left unchallenged the roots of these mental processes may not be

---

LET'S MOVE ON! IS IT REALLY THAT SIMPLE?

"We have come so far and slavery was hundreds of years ago. When will black people stop blaming the past and deal with the fact that their poor choices are the problem." This type of thought pattern comes from an inadequate understanding of the current state of the black community and how she got to where she is today. 72% of blacks are fatherless. Around 45% are never married. The family unit is collapsing as well as health and almost every other area. This can be directly attributed to the intentional separation of black families on the auction block, poor food supply of slaves and unhealed generational trauma. There is more than poor choices conducted in a mere lifetime at play.

---

realized but can be devastating to the daily interaction people have with one another due to faulty, inherited conceptualizations. Although the original tale is many times much more concentrated, the theories behind it remain.

For example, I attended a private Christian school throughout my childhood. In 5th grade, I remember we were about the close the day, just having left the playground. As I stood waiting, probably for my parents to pick me up from school, I could hear taunting voices behind me.

Legends die hard in popular mind,
while facts tend to languish in books.

Eldred Jones

They meanly declared, "Whoopi…Whoopi" then I could hear the chuckling continue. *(This was a joke against Whoopi Goldberg, dreadlocks and kinky hair)*. I had box braids in my hair and it was time for them to be redone but that was never an excuse for this type of treatment. It was clearly a sign that kinky textured hair was not as pretty as straighter, fine hair. And my heart sank as I felt those words. The 1156 tale continue to weave its philosophies in the minds of our children, black and white.

As far back as the first century, Africans were described as beasts. This would inevitably leave a negative stereotype in the minds of Europeans who had never been to Africa, creating a superiority complex in many. It also warrants the right to use them as property. **If Africans are not humans, then proprietorship becomes reasonable.** This sort of fallacious thinking would become a foundation for slavery. Imagine hearing these stories from respectable men; these were stories about a people much like monsters in classics such as the Odyssey or Gilgamesh, very contrastive to European peoples. Now the differential gap has increased in one's mind.

They are a people to fear and fear leads to the need to control when left untamed. No nose, no nostrils, huge faces, no tongues, unintelligent, beasts living with elephants, cannibals and people with the heads of dogs…This is the portrayal that resurged in the 1500s. Recently, I was given an opportunity to see how these established views are still subconscious realities of people. The irony is, it was at a justice luncheon in a beautiful suburban restaurant. I sat down next to two beautiful girls from one of the most sought after universities in America. One of which I could tell was very uncomfortable being at a table next to and across from three African Americans (my husband, myself and a matured lady).

I attempted to interact with this reserved student multiple times to bring ease. Further into the conversation the older black lady began to share how she purposely invited all cultures to work at her clinic. She went on to explain that her church recently changed its name as an outward expression of its desire to be cross-cultural.

The discomforted young lady then chimed in acknowledging her challenge to integrate with cultures differing her own and her tendency to bend toward Caucasians at her school's orientation. My speculations on her discomfort were confirmed.

It's crucial that we learn to face these types of challenges intentionally, avoiding forsaking our own GOD-given culture, while honing a willingness to integrate with others in the Body of Christ. This young lady was noticing her own preconceived notions about

---

OULADAH EQUIANO

Words of Wisdom from a Former Slave

Let the polished and haughty European recollect that his ancestors were once, like the Africans, uncivilized, and even barbarous. Did Nature make them inferior to their sons? And should they too have been made slaves? Every rational mind answers, No. Let such reflections as these melt the pride of their superiority into sympathy for the wants and miseries of their sable brethren, and compel them to acknowledge, that understanding is not confined to feature or colour. If, when they look round the world, they feel exultation, let it be tempered with benevolence to others, and gratitude to God, "who hath made of one blood all nations of men for to dwell on all the face of the earth; and whose wisdom is not our wisdom, neither are our ways his ways."

The Interesting Narrative of the Life of Olaudah Equiano

---

black Americans. We can learn from her example. It is vital that we join her in examining the racial perceptions (that may be prejudices in our hearts) due to limited experiences or a lack of understanding.

It is helpful to know these preconceptions are not random nor arbitrary, they are based on established moments in history. Another key moment that will help us trace racial tensions is the day slavery begin. We can identify exactly when and how it happened.

One act of injustice due to great need
or simple greed can evolve into a monstrous
institution, seemingly overnight.

THE MOMENT THAT BEGAN SLAVERY

Slavery began due to European need for labour subsequent to the Black Death (1347-51) (Reader 331). Prior to this, "in 1341 the King of Portugal, Afonso IV, declared the Canaries to be within Portugal's domain and dispatched a slave-raiding expedition to the archipelago.

In the decades that followed, Europeans of many nationalities joined forces to raid the Canary Islands for captives." (Reader 331)

One of the many lessons we can learn from historical accounts is that **we should never resort to immoral action as a solution to great need.** We should also deny ourselves of superfluous luxuries except they can be acquired through respectable means.

One act of injustice due to great need or simple greed can evolve into a monstrous institution, seemingly overnight. This is what transpired in the year 1436, in one slave purchase between the Portuguese and Africans on the Coast of West Africa. Consequently, slavery exponentially grew as other nations heard of slavery's potential financial gain. The unimaginable began to occur.

In 1444, "Portuguese merchants who previously had been scornful of the notion now applied to Henry for a licence to send trading voyages to Africa." (Reader 335) Although people knew slavery was drastically immoral, they still did it because of greed and financial gain. The more they did what was wrong, the more it became a cultural norm. What once seemed horrific now became acceptable. This same principle applies in our current times through injustices left uncontested.

It is amazing how slavery evolved into a formal, horrific institution due to one slave purchase. Within a few years a trade of 10 slaves turned into a trade of 230 slaves. In 1436, a Portuguese ship led by Goncalvez Baldaya, landed on the coast of West Africa, about 248 miles south of Cape Bojador (in Morocco).

Goncalvez sent two of his youth on horses to explore the land. As they journeyed inshore to find "villages or people" they were greeted by "nineteen men all banded together without any arms of offence or defence, but only assegais [short stabbing spears.]" (Reader 335) The young men then fought the nineteen men using their swords until the "late afternoon." Then they returned to the ship. Five years later (1441), another Spanish exploration led by Adam Goncalvez occurred. He led nine men inland, then joined with Portuguese explorer, Nuno Tristao to attack two African camps overnight.

This attack would become the springboard to hundreds of years of chattel slavery. The result of this attack was as follows, "four Africans were killed and ten taken prisoner." Out of the ten prisoners one learned Portuguese and guaranteed the Africans would replace him with five to six "slaves." The Portuguese returned him and two other slaves for the purchase of more slaves, plus items:

> "Antam Goncalvez received ten
> slaves for his captives, plus an oxhide
> shield, ostrich eggs (subsequently
> served to Prince Henry "as fres and

LITTLE MOMENTS

Sometimes we are convinced that the Little Moments don't really count. You know, the time you heard a parent talk about how violent and uneducated that "other" race is or the time friends bashed the "other" because he was too ethnic. These little moments have proven to change history.

as good as though they had been the eggs of any other domestic fowls") and "a little gold dust."") (Reader 335)

Once word spread of this purchase it sparked a profit-oriented attraction to slavery. Viewpoints began to drastically shift regarding the morality of this institution and what was previously strongly detested became socially acceptable by more businessmen, who began sending ships to purchase slaves.

In 1444 the unimaginable occurred, the first voyager to receive a "licence" to go to Africa was named Lancarote. He "took a fleet of six armed caravels to West Africa and returned with 230 slaves. This expedition marked the beginning of the West African slave trade as a part of European commerce." (Reader 335).

LUXURY AT SLAVE'S EXPENSE

As one looks in retrospect at slavery, the words of Equiano remain true. It is always dangerous when an economy begins to be supplemented, supported or primarily built on injustice. The continent of Africa was being depleted and exploited, not only in natural resources, but human resources were being diminished as Europe took "many of its young, strong, healthy people" by means of the slave trade.

Slavery was at its core about financial gain, as seen in Queen Elizabeth I's doubt when the concept was initially presented to her (according to the book *Hard Road to Freedom*). Yet still, when she was presented with the lucrative nature of enslaving Africans, she willingly supported this 'industry' with her own resources (Horton & Horton 22).

Slavery was being enforced strongly by the British Empire, becoming the fuel to a very plush lifestyle at the expense of Africans' physical and personal livelihood. In fact, by 1880 England "had overtaken Portugal, Spain, France and Holland, and were the indisputable moguls of the international slave ring. Slavery was so essential to the British economy that the government sought to protect it at all cost." (Burton 202)

Although slavery had become the norm to British people, it would never be normal to people of African descent. It is more than a page in history; it is a testimonial story line of a people, broken, traumatized and mistreated.

It was a deep injustice affecting an entire continent's well-being. It was a disruption to life itself, oftentimes ending in death. *Yet many continued to pretend as if they did not know the extent of devastation occurring for the sake of their daily comforts.*

Europe's economy eventually became so dependent on slavery that economists could not imagine the world without this institution. Even after slavery was abolished (in the 1880s) and laws were made to free slaves, it was not enough to stop the slave trade or domestic slavery in Africa. Instead, as other resources were found slavery increased.

The Europeans would need slaves to continue working in the new trade, palm vegetable oils. As nations sent law enforcement to the coast of Africa, the slave trade continued (Phillips 19). This was due to the "tons" of oil trade between England and Africa.

TRAUMA TO A CONTINENT: FIRST ACCOUNTS OF EUROPEAN SLAVERY

In a mere 34-year time span the landscape of an entire continent would be drastically changed by European colonization and the effects of slavery. As world powers began to see Africa's abundant range of resources they went on a domination treasure hunt. In this process, not only was African authority violated, but the prosperity of future generations would be broken. As centuries-old, established cultures were disrupted, the next generations had to relearn what was passed down for ages. This is the reality that African Americans are now facing explaining the long-standing breakdown of a displaced people group. In today's black community:

- 72% are fatherless
- 19% are college educated
- 27% are in poverty
- 57% of women are obese
- 38% of men are obese

LESSONS FROM HISTORY

When we build systems based on sinful behaviors, we find ourselves at a loss of Godly resources and must oftentimes start from a place of nothingness or spiritual poverty until we can find our way back home.

- ❖ 17% have less than a high school diploma
- ❖ 44% have HIV
- ❖ 41% of men have hypertension
- ❖ 45% of women have hypertension
- ❖ 30% aborted
- ❖ 69% have unintended pregnancies
- ❖ 44% of men have heart disease and stroke
- ❖ 48% of women have heart disease and stroke

Now let's compare that to the white community, while remembering that black Americans consist of only 12.3% of the population[7]. These are generational effects of intentionally breaking down a people's family unit:

Black Americans	Caucasian Americans
72% are Fatherless	20.7% are Fatherless
19% are College Educated	29.3% are College Educated
27% are in Poverty	11.6% are in Poverty
57% of Women are Obese	32.8% of Women are Obese
38% of Men are Obese	32.4% of Men are Obese
73% Graduated High School	87% Graduated High School
44% have HIV	26% have HIV
41% of men have Hypertension	33.9% of men have Hypertension

45% of women have Hypertension	31.3% of women have Hypertension
30% aborted	39% aborted
79 per 1000 had unintended pregnancies	33 per 1000 had unintended pregnancies

It is important to note this abrupt change of Africa. would become a psychologically, emotionally and physically traumatic experience across the second largest continent in the world. Although benefited by economic development in some ways, the African diaspora has experienced trouble since.

This points directly back to the colonization of Africa. As seen in the above statistics, this has caused financial, emotional, educational and family health issues, even hundreds of years down the line. During colonization, many people groups experienced the loss of liberty, autonomy and leadership. In fact,

"by as late as 1880, about as much as 80% of the continent of Africa was being ruled by her own kings, queens, clan and lineage heads, in empires, kingdoms, communities and polities of various sizes and shapes"

but in the year 1914 (34 years later)

"with the sole exception of Ethiopia and Liberia, the whole of Africa had been subjected to the rule of European powers in colonies of various sizes which were generally much larger

---

7 "African Americans are nearly twice the risk for a first-ever stroke than white people." Cdc.gov/heart.org

physically but often bore little or no relationship to the preexisting polities." (Boahen 1)

Imagine the effects this must have had on the African people, not just as a group but as individuals with life meaning, purpose and families. Suddenly their worlds were dominated, shaken by others they did not recognize. As they were taken to a New World they did not know, the memories became a distant daydream they would never see again.

AFRICAN VS. EUROPEAN SLAVERY

Some people would argue, But didn't Africans have slaves too? Before European colonization and slavery swiped across Africa, Africans had a servitude system but it was not chattel slavery. Chattel is "an item of intangible movable or immovable property except real estate, freehold, and things (as buildings) connected with real property; slave, bondsmen."[8] This could in part explain the initial willingness for Africans to sell their own into slavery. Little did they know of the monstrous level of atrocity about to be introduced to their people. This is not to say that all Africans were saints, because some continued selling their own for gain, even after seeing the trade was clearly inhumane. Nevertheless, African slavery was a different story than the chattel system enforced by Europeans. The key difference between African and European enslavement was the treatment and rights of slaves.

---

[8] Merriam-Webster Dictionary

African slavery was much less hostile:

"…Native-born slaves might be children of prisoners of war, those natives enslaved for committing some crime, or those sold by their relatives. Native-born and domestic (house) slaves customarily **could not be sold** (except for the commission of an especially heinous crime), **often inherited property** from the master, **married their free-born kinsmen,** and occasionally **became guardians** of the master's minor children. (Berry & Blassingame 4, bold added)

Africans had an entirely different concept of slavery based on civilized laws and treatment towards their slaves. These slaves had rights that European slaves could only dream of, such as owning property, marrying, and becoming legal guardians.

African slavery also differed from European slavery in that Africans were allowed days off, half days, their own land, commission, their own jobs and owned their own slaves (Berry and

THE NEW WORLD

A black perspective of The New World may be quite different than how whites recall it. For blacks it was more like A New Nightmare. It was a world of so many unfamiliarity's but not in a hopeful way. The Plymouth Ship and the Middle Passage were strikingly different existences.

Blassingame 5). There was a guarding of the marital unit between slaves and laws in place to ensure the safety of women for sexual crimes (Berry and Blassinggame 6). They were allowed the ability to assume offices in the government and work in the military. They were able to keep their dignity, not only as humans but also as leaders in the community.

As they were taken to a New World
they did not know, the memories
became a distant daydream they
would never see again.

Contrarily, European slaves were at a loss of any rights and were generally not respected as leaders in the community. Instead, they were considered holistically subservient to the Europeans (Berry and Blassingame 6).

Because the family unit was devastatingly ripped apart during European slavery, it is important to note that African slavery carried a tighter family dimension. Even when a person was enslaved their families (although free) would remain together, keeping a sense of unity amongst a people group and generational line (Berry and

Blassingame 5). This is key to dealing with the loss of identity in the African American community. If the family unit was kept intact both genealogical records would be easier to obtain and the valuable wisdom of former generations would have been available in building the next generation. Instead, there was at least some measure of loss in continuing the stories and family similarities that would have helped people of African descent to build--without starting from scratch.

Families enslaved by Europeans oftentimes never saw one another again. This happened to husband and wife, mother and child. There are no words to express the widespread sense of grief and loss this has caused. There were entire tribes becoming "depopulated"

African Slavery	European Slavery
Could not be sold	For Sale
Inherited Property	No Rights to Own
Married	Illegal to Marry
Became Guardians	No Legal Guardianship
Time Off	Worked Mercilessly
Their Own Jobs	Limited Jobs
Protected from Sex Crimes	Rampant Sexual Slavery
Civil Office Military Government Opportunities	No Civil Rights to Office, Voting or Military
Family Preservation	Family Split on Auction Blocks

affecting the landscape of people groups, such as the Ashanti and the Dahomey (Berry and Blessingame 7).

Equiano's Kidnapping

"One day, when all of our people were gone out to their works as usual, and only I and my dear sister were left to mind the house, two men and a woman got over our walls, and in a moment seized us both, and, without giving us time to cry out, or make resistance, they stopped our mouths, and ran off with us into the nearest wood. Here they tied our hands, and continued to carry us as far as they could, till night came on, when we reached a small house, where the robbers halted for refreshment, and spent the night…I began to cry out for their assistance: but my cries had no other effect than to make them tie me faster and stop my mouth, and then they put me into a large sack."

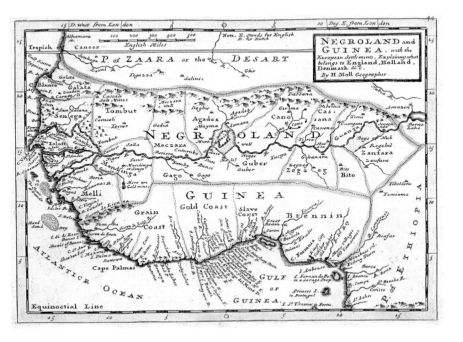

Figure 4   This is a 1736 map of the Gold Coast, where gold was originally traded as the largest commodity but then slaves became the richest "resource."

This would have been very problematic to the strength of African society- their strongest rulers and people were being stripped from their land and the family unit was being disrupted.   What these people have suffered is more than an emotional loss. There is also the loss of an oral culture, from which Africans have learned how their people group has operated for ages, how to cure sicknesses common to family lines, what to look out for based on past history and how to overcome the challenges of generations before- this knowledge is powerfully invaluable.

Because European slavery was based on the mentality that slaves were inhuman, there was a justification in brutalizing the black family unit.

Family is a common thread through the communities of people of African descent (Horton & Horton 16). The importance of family ties and the consideration of community as family has been pivotal to our survival through years of injustice through means as slavery, segregation, Jim Crow laws, and racism.

IMAGINE THE PAIN

Have you ever experienced sudden loss- from the pain of losing a best friend to the loss of a child, the spectrum of grief we endure can be overwhelming. This understanding of what it is like to experience loss helps us to bemoan the pain of others. No matter our complexion, we can relate to a missed hug, phone call or lack of affection. We can relate to an unexplained medical diagnosis, mental health issues of a family member or receiving a rejection letter from our dream job. From that stance of pain, we may not know what it's like to be stripped of a family, but we can mourn the loss of other people groups as we consider our own loss. What must they be feeling as they realize how far removed they are from Family Trends? How would you feel if you were in their shoes? We don't have to have all the answers to "be with" one another in compassionate love!

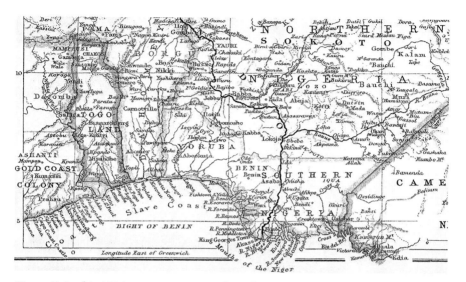

Figure 5 In this 1896 map, one can see the Ashanti people, where great leaders such as Harriet Tubman were from, which is directly in the Gold/Slave Coast."

Even when a person was enslaved their families (although free) would remain together, keeping a sense of unity amongst a people group and generational line. Understanding this is key to dealing with the loss of identity in the African American community.

But this emphasis further reveals the significant trauma occurring when slaves such as Equiano were suddenly ripped from home. Although African Americans were able to maintain family ties, a lot has been loss due to slavery. The cultural norms and lessons they would have gained have in some senses weakened the family unit in ways that statistics have glaringly proven.

This is why the Plymouth text was so uninspiring for me, a black high school student, who only saw dark Middle Passage ships---from a paradise of palm trees, mango juice and happy black faces content to live a simple, joyful life we were brought to horror. Our lives were centered around family, around love. This was the story I longed to

---

WHEN ATTACHMENT NEVER HAPPENS

Slavery stopped proper attachment between mothers and their children, fathers and their seed. When that occurs in an individual's life detachment can become the norm. According to the great children's psychologist, Dr. Karyn Purvis, "attachment" is "the interpersonal bond between a child and his or her parent or caretaker. A child who felt consistently safe and nurtured by a reliable caretaker in early life will become securely attached." (The Connected Child, pg. 48) When this does not happen the child does not learn how to build strong, healthy relationships and may pass on these behaviors to his children. What happens when an entire community has suffered detachment and trauma for many years? The healing must begin.

---

hear but never did. This is the history we all need to behold if we are ever to understand the anger in America's dark children's eyes.

REFLECTION QUESTIONS

1. How can knowing what colonization was like from an African perspective begin to help you gain more compassion for people of African descent?
2. How can the dismantling of African families have a domino effect on African American families today? Today 72% of black families are fatherless.
3. What were you taught about black history and colonization in school? Do you feel that you were equipped to understand the history from an educated and relational level?
4. Can you relate to family breakdown in your own life or the life of a friend? How did this make you feel?
5. "Be happy with those who are happy, and weep with those who weep." (Romans 12:15) How can this Scripture help us bringing healing to our current pains? How might feeling the historical and current pains of the black community be helpful?

Chapter 3
Middle Passages

*For them, the New World was not a dream, it was a nightmare.
And these displaced peoples are still living on the shores their ancestors
were forced into horrific domain.*

AN UNLIKELY BAPTISM

Baptism is an ancient part of the church experience, reaching back to 1st century Christianity. In fact, John the Baptist—who leaped in the womb when his mother Elizabeth greeted pregnant Mary—led a baptism-movement that would change history. Jesus called him the greatest prophet to ever exist and John's voice prepared the way for the world to receive their Savior. We all have varying perspectives and experiences with baptism. For some the idea of family comes to mind as we gather aunties, uncles, grandparents, friends and dear loved ones into a small yet happy church festivity. Our sweet baby is about to baptized into the church.

For others, we imagine a worn picture hanging from our grandmother's mantle, spirit-filled black women shouting fervently by a river side. Hats tilted to the side, hands adorned with trembling

The Amistad Mutiny

During the month of August 1839, reports were circulating up and down the eastern coast of the United States about a "mysterious long black schooner" sighted at sea. This ship was a Spanish schooner, Amistad, which had sailed from Havana for Port Principe, Cuba, on June 28, 1839. The Amistad carried, in addition to its crew, fifty-four African slaves. Four nights after leaving Havana the Africans, led by Cinqueé, mutinied, killing the captain and three of the crew. For nearly two months the Africans attempted to force the remaining members of the crew to sail the Amistad back to Africa. On August 26, 1839, Cinque and a few other Africans went ashore for supplies near Montauk Point on Long Island, New York. Soon after, the Amistad was illegally seized by the United States Navy. Cinque and his fellow countrymen were imprisoned and taken to New Haven to await trial before the next Circuit Court at Hartford...

The case against the Africans was argued by United States District Attorney Holabird whose position was that of the Spanish Government and American proslavery interests – that the Africans were slaves (property), and had committed murder...

The Amistad Mutiny

This order was sent before the court could assemble at New Haven on January 7, 1840, to further consider the Amistad case. When the New Haven court affirmed the decision of the Hartford court—that the Africans were freemen (not property or criminals) who had fought to regain their lost freedom—the United States Secretary of State ordered an appeal. Now the case was before the United States Supreme Court.

The legal counsel for the Africans, sensing the broad historical significance of this fight for freedom, realized the necessity of enlisting the aid of an individual who epitomized many of the idealistic qualities associated with the best of American character. They found this person in former President John Quincy Adams. Adams, then a Congressman from Massachusetts, eloquently argued the case before the Supreme Court and on March 8, 1841, the Africans were set free. The next year the Africans returned to their homeland, Sierra Leone."

tambourines and the sound of shouting fills the still images' atmosphere. We are going down by the riverside where all our sins are washed away, entering into glory one day!

And for those who grew up in a small Baptist church like me (practically born on the first pew) childhood memories swell with these emotionally sacred moments. That day when you gave your heart to Christ, confessed Him as your Savior and were unashamed for the world to know. Baptism was more than a religious experience, it was personal. Yet no one could deny the tradition of it all.

The day I was baptized is etched upon my memory as a memorial of my parent's passed on faith, my own dedication to the Lord at the age of four, and my desire to exhibit this deep passion. The pulpit was small yet powerful, two choir stands erected on either side; so many memories were made in that tiny community church. But at the height of the scene was a baptismal pool where our old past, although mine was a mere three years, was washed away forever. *I was saved!*

Many years prior, our ancestors were baptized as well. This baptism was of a different sort. It was not by choice. It was not happy. There was no service. Or celebrating family members. Ironically, it was a baptism immersed in water. The Atlantic Ocean began to swallow up each "passenger" including their family structure and happy memories on rich African soil where kings and queens were demoted to a pauper's life. In a moment's notice, they were chained and forced into servitude, never to be seen again; some had never even seen a large body of water or a boat. But now, immersed in the baptism of trauma, disease and barbaric treatment the shocking reality settled in. This nightmare was not a dream. It was the middle passage.

By some divine act of grace they made it to the New World. Our ancestors lived an Agonizing Life span so we could celebrate a more joyful type of immersion. Family Intact. Heads Held High. As we proudly raise up the next generation…No wonder baptism is so rich for the black community!

The Middle Passage was four centuries of the importation of human beings as property from Africa, across the Atlantic Ocean then to the Caribbean and America.

DISCOVERING THE MIDDLE PASSAGE

The Middle Passage was four centuries of the importation of human beings as property from Africa, across the Atlantic Ocean then to the Caribbean and America. There could have been as many as "13 million slave(s) (that) left Africa for the Atlantic." (Reader 380)

Not only was the Middle Passage a "journey" across the Atlantic Ocean, it was one of excruciating difficulty for Africans packed together on slave ships. Although some claim that the Middle Passage was only a couple hundred years, the ramifications of this horrific voyage lasted well beyond four hundred years. 13 million Africans were transported from the coast of Africa to America and the aftermath of this traumatic experience can still be seen and felt today.

These millions of transported Africans represent four generations (400 years), four times longer than the average lifetime. Upon knowing the details of this "passage" the level of pain and rippling effects this has is astronomical, for both descendants of slaves and their masters.

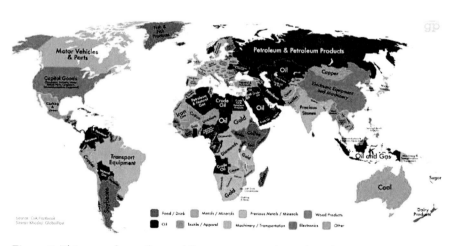

Figure 6 This map shows the world's most commonly exploited resources. Notice the richness of Africa's natural resources in comparison with the remainder of the world. Taken from www.globalpost.com

Figure 7 This map zooms into the many resources of the continent of Africa. Taken from www.globalpost.com

Figure 8 *This Slave Ship was given to the House of Commons in 1790 and 1790. Evidence of the brutalizing nature of the slave trade.*

SLAVE IMPORTATIONS TO THE NEW WORLD				
	Edward E. Dunbar	R.R. Kuczynshki	Philip D. Curtin	J. E. Inikori
16th Century	887,500		241,400	
17th Century	2,750,000		1,341,100	
18th Century	7,000,000		6,051,700	
19TH Century	3,250,000		1,898,400	
Total	**13,887,500**	**14,650,000**	**9,566,100**	**9,566,100+**

Table 1 The numbers in this chart are based on recorded censuses of slave importations based on the research of the four demographers and historians listed above. As one can see, there is a lot of conflict over how many slaves were actually imported.

Considering the fact that one isolated traumatic event can cause severe damage to a child or an adult in their lifetime, helps clarify the magnitude of the Middle Passage. If the rippling effects of being bullied, verbally abused, sexually molested or racially attacked can take a lifetime to overcome, then imagine the recuperation process of an entire people group. When comparing a people's emotions to a human soul, this is better understood. The soul is one's mind, will and emotions. In fact, it can be argued that the soul of African Americans has been brought into a sort of post traumatic syndrome and the soul of Caucasian Americans has settled into passive denial of the years gone by.

Both the issues of blacks and whites are deep rooted pains of the mind, emotional life and even bodies of individuals. The symptomatic evidence of these effects can be seen in every overt and covert racial encounter experienced in America today.

America as a whole appears to be in a state of deep trauma, "a painful emotional experience or shock, often producing a lasting psychic effect, and sometimes, a neurosis[9]."

TRAUMA OF THE PASSAGE

The Middle Passage was "a painful emotional experience or shock producing a lasting psychic effect…" It was **traumatic intentional violence to the soul of a nation (people group).** It included millions witnessing unheard of violence over hundreds of years, "sustained discrimination, poverty, and ensuing chaotic life conditions." Studies have proven this to have passed down to both African Americans and Hispanics,

POST TRAUMATIC SLAVE SYNDROME

Author and professor, Joy DeGruy Leary brilliantly coined the term, Post Traumatic Slave Syndrome, She asks, "...is it probable that significant numbers of African slaves experienced a sufficient amount of trauma to warrant a diagnosis of PTSD?" (DeGruy pg. 113) Could this be why current statistics are so bleak in the black community?

---

[9] (Websters College Dictionary Fourth Edition 1532).

who have higher rates of post-traumatic stress disorder and "live with chronic stress and do not have a regular source of healthcare"[10]

The soul is one's mind will and emotions. In fact, it can be argued that the soul of African Americans has been brought into a sort of post traumatic syndrome and the soul of many Caucasian Americans has settled into passive denial of the years gone by.

The Middle Passage was beyond inhumane. And just as the only way to stop trauma is through intervention, the same must be realized when dealing with our national adversary, racism. The fact that humans were humiliated to the extent of being treated worse than animals must be faced, it should no longer go ignored or be seen as "someone else's" problem. Wise handling and acknowledgement of wrong is greatly needed. This will take the willingness to educate ourselves on a guilt-ridden past.

---

[10](www.nonviolenceandsocialjustice.org/FAQs/What-is-Trauma/41/)

The Middle Passage not only physiologically removed a people group from their home land, it "ravaged black Africa like a brush fire, wiping out images and values in one vast carnage." (Franklin & Moss 49)

America as a whole, appears to be in a state of deep trauma "a painful emotional experience of shock, often producing a lasting psychic effect, and sometimes, a neurosis."

It was not a page of a history book, meaningless dates nor extraneous information; it is the painful, emotional stories of millions of men, women, boys and girls unexpectedly stripped from everything they knew into a mental hellacious world. Again, for them, the New World was not a dream; it was a nightmare. And these displaced peoples are still living on the very shores their ancestors were unjustly forced into a horrific domain. This "brush fire" would kill many and leave others as lifelong captives, never to see "home" again.

For many, this brush fire was never brought into subjection, it would burn upon their souls until their open caskets welcomed them to another home.

These were more than survivors, they were heroes, representing a displaced people, coming to build another man's land. They prayed, they sang, they quoted words from their homeland while on that boat for months, tied to the person next to them, women climbing to the top of the boat for a moment of air-only to be raped by lustful, demented captors.

This was a fire full of the wild flames of hatred and its soot remains on the souls of its people today. The soot is pasty and can only be understood by deep compassion. It takes time and more than a listening ear. It takes a listening heart.

The soot speaks of years of hopelessness, isolation, sickness, suicide, whippings, fear, rape and mental abuse. The isolation of the

Middle Passage was an unbearable existence, yet somehow endured by these strong men and women. These were more than survivors, they were heroes, representing a displaced people, coming to build another man's land.

They prayed, they sang, they quoted words from their homeland while on that boat for months at a time, tied to the person next to them, women climbing to the top of the boat for a moment of air—only to be raped by lustful, demented captors. All while their men, perhaps a husband or a brother watched helplessly, unable to fight back. Some threw themselves off the side of the boat into shark filled waves eager for yet more blood from the bodies of those in utter desperation. This is the soot that must be uplifted by blacks and recognized by whites if America is to be healed of this deep neurosis.

OVERPACKING HUMAN GOODS

The conditions and brutal treatment on these boats was worse than typically imagined. Overpacking, for example, was a major problem. It was really bad, to the extent that even the nominal number of slaves on a ship was unmentionable, but these numbers were increased by over a hundred when ships sent off across the Atlantic Ocean. One writer describes it as comparable to "the Holocaust for its callous inhumanity." Imagine a space so tight that "not a metre of space is left vacant" and "an extra shelf" must be built to add more slaves (Reader 389). We build "extra shelves" to pack containers in our laundry room or linen closet, not to place people on a six to nine month trip. But this is how slaves were treated on the journey across the Atlantic.

Furthermore, when laws were finally set into place, on the spacing of slaves, to limit "over packing" in ships (in 1713), the size determined **was still smaller than "most coffins."** Unfortunately, ship "captains earned commission on the slaves they landed" causing them to pack ships full "gambling for maximum returns." (Reader 389) These laws were completely ignored by some captains, who wanted more profit by packing as much human property as possible across the ocean. The slaves were considered objectified "cargo" and ""black people of every description was chained together" below-decks in the hold of the ship for six to eight weeks." (Horton & Horton 16) Former slave, Ouladah Equiano, provides a first-hand account of Middle Passage overpacking:

> "The stench of the hold while we were on the coast
> was so intolerably loathsome that it was   dangerous
> to remain there for any time, and some of us had
> been permitted to stay on the deck for the fresh air;
> but now that the whole ship's cargo were confined
> together, and the heat of the climate, added to the
> number in **the ship**, which **was so crowded that each
> had scarcely room to run himself**, almost suffocated
> us." (Horton & Horton 16)

In an account of the ship, *Brookes,* "over 600 slaves" were on it as human cargo prior to a law ruling that "up to 451 slaves" could be carried upon a slave ship if using the following dimensions, "a space six feet by one foot four inches...for each adult man, five feet ten inches by one foot for each adult woman, five feet by one foot two inches for each boy, and four feet six inches by one foot for each girl" (Horton & Horton 18). There were laws made by the British to enforce spacing on the ships, but no law would ever make this injustice acceptable nor humane.

HEALTH EPIDEMIC OF THE PASSAGE
Another aspect of the Middle Passage was the deadly "stench" of

WE HURT FOR THE JEWISH HOLOCAUST

I remember reading The Diary of Anne Frank and being heart-broken over her situation. As a Middle School student, her story and the story of the Jewish Holocaust gripped my heart. Yet I've found that some Caucasians state they do not get the black dilemma due to not being black. They don't feel called to reconciliation or they do not relate to our struggles. To some degree this may be true, but we all have one commonality- the ability to feel. We can feel for a child who broke his arm, a widow who lost her spouse or a couple whose home was demolished. Saying that we don't or can't relate because we are not in someone else's shoes is never a good excuse for a lack of empathy.

these trips, described by Equiano as "suffocating" when combined with the heat. The emotional trauma of a person being suddenly stripped of his home and loved ones, thrown into the physical trauma of being overpacked, chained into the bottom of a disease, heat-ridden ship, barely able to breath for months was the atrocious norm of the Middle Passage.

Surely, this horrendous experience would be etched into Equiano's mind forever; fortunately he was given the privilege to write about it in his autobiography. He also described the horrible smell as "intolerably loathsome" and the heat as so bad that it "almost suffocated us." This was amid the utter shock of seeing both a ship and Europeans for the first time in his life. This was not due to an ironically isolated response or because Africans were uneducated about Europeans. The same would have occurred in any person of any race when faced with similar conditions (Horton & Horton 16).

Outside of the obvious mental turmoil and years of trauma this ship had to have on the slaves, there were serious physical, unaddressed health conditions. These slaves were bound by shackles for eight hours a day, eating once in the morning and again eight hours later according to Alexander Falconbridge, "a British surgeon" who "made the voyage from West Africa to the West Indies thirty years after Equiano's journey." They lay there in tight conditions for all of those eight hours in the unquenchable stench Equiano previously described. Their "meals" were made up of "horsebeans, boiled to the consistence of a pulp; of boiled yams and rice, and sometimes of a small quantity of beef and pork." (Horton & Horton 18)

This was obviously not enough nutrients and no-where near a

balanced meal for humans struggling to survive in a situation that would already weaken the immune system and inevitably attract diseases or viruses.

Because of poor food supply and unsanitary conditions, they were very prone to illness. Many died from "disease, malnutrition, mistreatment, or lack of fresh air." It took an extremely strong mind to endure this passage, let alone maintain any level of sanity (Horton & Horton 18). Franklin and Moss provide a detailed description of the different types of disease on slave ships:

> "It was doubtless the crowded conditions on the vessels that so greatly increased the incidence of disease and epidemics during the voyage to America. **Smallpox** was one of the dread diseases of the period, and one experienced observer remarked that few ships that carried slaves escaped without it. Perhaps even more deadly than smallpox was flux, a

IMAGINE THE SHOCK

Imagine what it was like to have never seen a ship or a white person and this is your introduction. What do you do? How do you feel? What do you think the ocean is? Are the white people ghosts? Are you in hell? Many Africans had these questions running through their minds until able to hear the truth from a slave who already was brought to the Americas.

frequently fatal malady from which whites on board the slave ships were apparently spared. **Hunger strikes** at times aggravated unfavorable health conditions and induced illnesses where previously there had been none. **The filth and stench** caused by close quarters and disease brought on more illness, and the mortality rate increased accordingly. Perhaps not more than half the slaves shipped from Africa ever became effective workers in the New World. **Many of those who did not die of disease or commit suicide by jumping overboard were permanently disabled by the ravages of some dread disease or by maiming,** which often resulted from struggling against the chains. Small wonder that one trader who arrived at Barbados with 372 of his original 700 slaves was moved to remark: "No gold-finders can endure so much noisome slavery as they do who carry Negroes; for those have some respite and satisfaction, but we endure twice the misery; and yet by the mortality our voyages are ruin'd and we pine and fret ourselves to death, to think that we should undergo so much misery, and take so much pains to so little purpose." (Franklin & Moss 44-45, Bold Emphasis Added)

Slaves had to endure through diseases like smallpox, flux, sickness (due to hunger strikes) and becoming disabled (due to illness). It is a dismal thought to ponder the extent of sickness on these ships. Some of the other types of sicknesses were "scurvy, diarrhea, and various skin diseases" (William & Harris 128-129). By the year 1788 surgeons were legislated to be on ships, but conditions were so horrific that this only helped minimally. According to John Newton's account, they were stuck in this strait for as long as "nine or ten" months at a time. He stated, "Thus they must sit, walk, and lie, for many months (sometimes nine or ten), without any mitigation or relief…" (Reader 389).

WOMEN AND CHILDREN

There were also women and children on these ships. Although these women "were often allowed to remain above decks for longer periods of time because they were believed to be less dangerous" they had to be faced with the psychological horror of the constant threat of sexual abuse by their white male captors on the ship. The youth were especially at threat while on the ship, given more time as women above ship, they were constantly exposed to these lust-filled men (Horton & Horton 19). To this day black women have to fight through the belittling portrayals of themselves as sexual images as opposed

HEALTH REPORTS

Have you ever been sick or given a bad doctor report? The smallest cold, a runny nose or a nauseous stomach can be annoying. We will take pills, try new remedies and listen to folk tales to stop the discomfort. Stronger reports are even more scary. Imagining your own sick days may help bring emotions to how slaves may have felt on the Middle Passage.

to white women who are more easily perceived as "decent" women. This has catastrophic effects on the identity and self-esteem of women if not interrupted by deep healing.

Due to overpacking and insanitary conditions, children on the ships would many times fall into "tubs" full of human feces as this is where the captives had to excrete (Equiano 38). This type of cruel treatment towards children was obviously unacceptable. Simply imagining the horror a mother, a father or a loved one watching helplessly is heart wrenching. The very ones who should have been able to protect were now held captive themselves.

BARBARIC TREATMENT

As if sickness was not an adequate amount of suffering, the treatment of the slaves was nothing short of barbaric. The first encounter a slave had with dehumanizing treatment was capture. In the case of Equiano, he was kidnapped and stripped from his family, then separated from his last family connection, his sister (who was kidnapped with him). These slaves were thrown into sacks and taken to slave ports in West Africa. They would then experience an aloneness many will never feel in a lifetime. Equiano describes entry into the Middle Passage with exceptionally vivid quality:

> "The first object which saluted my eyes when I arrived on the coast was the sea, and a slave-ship, which was then riding at anchor, and waiting for its cargo. These filled me with astonishment, which was soon converted into terror, which I am yet at a loss to describe, nor the then feelings of

my mind. When I was carried on board I was immediately handled, and tossed up, to see if I were sound, by some of the crew; and **I was now persuaded that I had gotten into a world of bad spirits, and that they were going to kill me. Their complexions too differing so much from ours, their long hair, and the language they spoke, which was very different from any I had ever heard, united to confirm me in this belief. Indeed, such were the horrors of my views and fears at the moment, that, if ten thousand worlds had been my own, I would have freely parted with them all to have exchanged my condition with that of the meanest slave in my own country.** When I looked round the ship too, and saw a large furnace of copper boiling, and a multitude of black people of every description chained together, every one of their countenances expressing dejection and sorrow, I no longer doubted of my fate, and, quite overpowered with horror and anguish, I fell motionless on the deck and fainted."
(Equiano 33-34, bold added)

This passage illustrates the heart of Equiano's emotions, "horror and anguish" filled him to the point of fainting. The shock was too overwhelming. For the first time he would see white people, a ship, and an ocean. He thought he must have been taken by evil spirits in another world. His mind could not understand what was occurring. He would also experience terrifying sounds described as "the shrieks of the women, and the groans of the dying" (Equiano 38). All of his senses seemed to be overtaken by excruciating pain.

His captors were committing cruelty for the sake of cruelty, revealing the depth of evil that can be honed in a soul left uncontrolled. For example, Equiano described how they would see the white men eat fish and when finish, throw the left-over fish over board while the slaves watched crying out for food to eat. When slaves tried to take some, they were whipped by these men (Equiano 38). The captains would also try to impart extreme fear tactics to make examples out of slaves. C.L.R. James proposes that they believed "that blacks

---

RELATING TO ALONENESS

There's probably been a time or two you've felt aloneness, like being in a room full of people but not connected, different from everyone else around you, unable to break into a clique. We all have different ways of coping with aloneness but the fact remains, we need one another. We are placed in families and communities for a reason but when this is broken we can go through mild to severe depression. Knowing what it is like to feel alone can help you imagine what it must have felt like for slaves like Equiano to be thrown into a strange new world, traumatically separated from anyone or anything familiar.

---

would only obey in the face of force and terror." (William & Harris 129-130).

In fact, the events of the Middle Passage were so horrific that slaves literally began to believe everything from white men's shoes to food was from African bodies and skin. Even beginning to believe or think this reveals the depth of mistreatment blacks experienced. One 1787 ship visitor expressed:

> In their own country they have themselves heard such dreadful tales of how the slaves are treated…that one is appalled when one hears them. **I was once asked by a slave, in complete earnest, if the shoes I was wearing had been made of Black Skin, since he had observed that they were the same colour as his skin.** (Reader 388, bold added)

SENSES & TRAUMA

What happens when our senses are overtaken—all of them at once—by trauma? This occurs with rape and physically violated victims. There is a sense of complete loss of control. Smells, colors, tastes can evoke painful memories. The same occurs for many blacks today, as they remember the past and live in harsh conditions.

The conduct described caused slaves to rise in massive slave rebellions, revealing the determination and level of strength these men, women and children still embodied. Slaves did not succumb to maltreatment without a fight or at least an attempt to revolt; in fact, the sailors had to be careful not to be harmed by slaves due to their determination in the midst of grave conditions. These slaves were described as ones who "[fight] like wild beasts" (Horton & Horton 18-19) and movies such as *Amistad* reveal an animated illustration of such moments. But when slaves rebelled they were treated even worse, as on "an English ship" when one woman rebelled. She was "hanged by her thumbs, whipped, slashed with knives, and allowed to bleed to death" simply to "make a special example of the woman" (Horton & Horton 20).

THE POWER OF EDUCATION

As one considers the Middle Passage and trials of enslaved Africans it is easy to see how America would continue to face racial dilemmas. Unfortunately, many still remain uneducated on how much Africans experienced and for how long. There is oftentimes a forgive and forget, quickly-let-go mentality in some white and black Americans. There is a dismissal, refusal, a neglect to realize how deeply the current generation of those of African descent have been effected by slavery. There is also a miseducation, or lack thereof, of how deeply slavery has affected the white community without realization. The Middle Passage has impacted generations of white Americans, who are now descendants of former slave masters.

We were baptized in the fire of the Middle Passage but baptized in a new fire, the fire of love. There is hope but there's a process to getting to that point. Some whites desire for blacks to forgive, but it is important to understand exactly what is being forgiven. Without this knowledge these issues spring up cyclically and healing is never realized.

It will greatly bless many blacks if the white community learns their history communicating words of compassion, care and respect. **One cannot forgive someone for something he or she does not fully understand and cannot ask for forgiveness in areas he or she does not comprehend. A blanket, "I'm sorry" and "Let's focus on what we have in common" has proven to not be enough.**

Slaves were taken on horrifying trips across the Atlantic Ocean for hundreds of years. This problem was not created in a moment and will not be resolved in a moment's notice. Therefore, we must be willing to go on a Reverse Journey across the Middle Passage, walking hand and hand through a thorough process of releasing

---

FEAR TACTICS & FEAR OF BLACKS

C.L.R. James proposes that white captors believed "that blacks would only obey in the face of force and terror." Why were the captors afraid of blacks when they were the ones acting barbarically? This same pattern continues today. Blacks are assumed to be "thugs," "criminals," and "thieves." They are followed around stores and watched more cautiously when they have the history of being mistreated. It is impossible to both love and fear simultaneously. We must overcome fear with love.

educated forgiveness, that is, if we want to see America thrive on a soulish level once and for all.

REFLECTION QUESTIONS

1. Did you learn something new from this Chapter regarding the Middle Passage? What did you learn?

2. If you are of another race, how can you begin to have more compassion for African Americans whose ancestors have experienced slavery? Compassion is defined as "Sorrow for the sufferings or trouble of another or others, accompanied by an urge to help; deep sympathy." This is not the same as feeling sorry for a person.

3. Sympathy is "to share or understand the feelings or ideas of another." Has there ever been a time you have felt similar feelings of pain, anger, belittling or helplessness slaves may have felt on the Middle Passage? What were those feelings?

4. How do you think slaves on the Middle Passage felt through inexpressible mistreatment and heavy persecution?

5. If you are African American, have you been thoroughly educated about the Middle Passage? How can you ensure that you are educated regarding your past?

6. If you are African American, can you see problems in the African American community that may have stemmed from the Middle Passage?

7. If you are Caucasion, have you been thoroughly educated about the Middle Passage? How can you get educated about this part of American history?
8. If you are Caucasion, can you see problems in the White community that may have stemmed from the Middle Passage?
9. Take time to forgive the white people who hurt blacks in the Middle Passage and take time to release forgiveness to your own people group for hurting blacks (if you are white).

Chapter 4
American Slavery

We must feel the impact of this great atrocity, Slavery, before we can deeply care about the injustices of the African American community... but how can we feel unless we first know the storyline?

THE MOMENT THAT CHANGED HOW I LEAD

I remember believing I was a great leader. And maybe I was *for the most part?* But, I was taught to lead with an Authoritative model. This meant that I had control and I was to tell the people what to do, I was to make sure they knew who was in charge no matter what. Now, there are times we need to operate in authority but telling an oldest child to lead this way...well you know where that can go!

Of course, like most young leaders, I learned this lesson through experience. **I must gain relational permission before I take positional authority.** I learned a lot through living my life and studying slavery. I began to see how much slave mentalities continue to lace through our culture today. This sickened me to my core. It changed the way I live my life.

You know you have a slave mentality when you believe the people

"So what is trauma? Trauma is an injury caused by an outside, usually violent, force, event or experience. We can experience this injury physically, emotionally, psychologically, and/or spiritually...If a trauma is severe enough it can distort our attitudes and beliefs. Such distortions often result in dysfunctional behaviors, which can in turn produce unwanted consequences. If one traumatic experience can result in distorted attitudes, dysfunctional behaviors and unwanted consequences, this pattern is magnified exponentially when a person repeatedly experiences severe trauma...it is much worse when the traumas are caused by human beings.

The slave experience was one of continual, violent attacks on the slave's body, mind and spirit...In the face of these injuries, those traumatized adapted their attitudes and behaviors to simply survive, and these adaptations continue to manifest today.."

Post Traumatic Slave Syndrome by Dr. Joy DeGruy Leary

"under" you are happily submitting to your leadership. But in reality, they feel oppressed, torn down, belittled, emasculated and used. This thought dug deep down into my heart before I considered how it applied to multitudes of others. Had I adopted a slave mentality from former generations?

I must gain relational permission
before I take positional authority.

Did I even take the time to ask those following me how my leadership "felt"? It should not feel like they are in bondage if I am leading graciously. As a leader, I learned the value of taking myself through vigorous self-checks to ensure I was not abusing the willing hearts of those in my care with too strong of an approach… all because I assumed they would not follow without "really strong authority."

In slavery, the time came when the Confederates felt the slaves were happy and even benefited from slavery. They felt the slaves needed them. But this was out of a superiority complex that had been forged into their racist mindsets. The slaves did not need them. This controlling viewpoint had become a stronghold of the south. They saw the slaves as their people. And then this concept began to creep into the American community, sometimes the church, sometimes the family, sometimes with how we addressed "really strong" black children that we believed needed heavier discipline. We got stuck in a race to be "owner" or "master" while neglecting the importance of "friend."

And it all began with slavery.

It's so important that we first seek to see the value of those we are trying to bless before trying to save them from their plight.

HOW SLAVERY BEGAN IN THE AMERICAS

It is not common knowledge that the commencement of slavery in the United States did not happen immediately nor expeditiously. There was a process that caused slavery to evolve. Specific situations opened doors to the moral degradation of this new nation's society. One incident led to slavery; emerging out of the institution of indentured servanthood--"in those years African and European indentured servants might work side by side." It is important to note that "Africans could purchase their freedom through work just as Europeans." *(Up From Slavery)* But what was the turning point from this seemingly fair playing ground of work-life into the horrific establishment known today as slavery? In 1641 what may have appeared as a minor legal change or isolated incident sparked hundreds of years of misery for the black community:

> "An early sign of the changes to come occurred in 1641. A Virginia court sentenced three indentured servants who had ran away from their masters. Two of the men were white and each sentenced to an extra year of service. The one black man was sentenced to a lifetime of servitude. This was the first known case of enslavement in Virginia." (Up from Slavery)

HEAR TO HELP BUT DOING DAMAGE

A few years ago a group of white missionaries joined us, a group of inner city black missionaries, to have a talk about how to reach Atlanta's urban core. They wanted to "help" and were trying to help Alabama's urban core, but were discovering racial barriers. These barriers are there because for years the black community had seen white Christians come in as superior "Savior" types without honoring her history or culture. It's so important that we first seek to see the value of those we are trying to bless before trying to save them from their plight. Perhaps the learning could go both ways. Let's seek to be relational while being missional.

This act of slavery is the root to how slavery began in America. It only took one black man being sentenced to a lifetime of slavery for an entire institution to begin. Compassionately and intuitively looking at how "each black man" is treated in our modern times will help us to never repeat the heart of such historical fallacies.

It only took one black man sentenced
to a lifetime of slavery
for an entire institution to begin.

AMERICA NEEDS THIS CHAPTER

We only have time to briefly survey a few of slavery's horrors such as #1 the raping and murder of women, #2 animalistic treatment of children, and #3 stripping husbands of their natural protector role. Please keep in mind, the accounts reported in this text are provided to gain a general understanding, yet only touch the surface concerning the enormous institution. There are so many aspects of this establishment that it would take multiple publications for me to give this topic the justice deserved. But the descriptions found here should be enough to bring to understanding why we are currently facing unresolved racial issues, even after hundreds of years in emancipation. Such trauma must be intentionally addressed in the hearts of both American whites and blacks before we are able to move forward.

THE TREATMENT OF WOMEN:
AN UNDERGROUND SEXUAL INDUSTRY

Understanding the treatment of women during slavery can help to understand America's current treatment and perspective of black women, including our current views and media portrayals. This chapter also includes Questions of Meditation to help reflect on how slavery origins affect us today.

During slave times, women, across the board, were not given the same rights as men.

Slavery occurred well before America's feminist movement in the 1960s but work was beginning to occur in the early 1800s for women's rights in conjunction with the Abolitionist Movement.

Without question, slave women were treated with even more contempt and less rights than white women of their day. It is hard to imagine the difficulty of living as a black women during this time period, yet we will try to, at the least, identify with some of the emotions these women were experiencing. This is key to understanding the current emotions and mental experience of black women.

It is hard to imagine the difficulty of living as a black woman during this time period, yet we will try to, at the least, identify with some of the emotions these women were experiencing.

THE DANGER OF UNFAIR SENTENCING

It only took one black man being sentenced to a lifetime of slavery for an entire institution to begin. Today many people do not realize the national statistics for black male incarceration. While 1 in every 15 African American males are incarcerated, 1 in every 106 while males are incarcerated (americanprogress.org) This is not because blacks tend to be criminals more than whites. The NAACP reports that "5 times as many Whites are using drugs as African Americans, yet African Americans are sent to prison for drug offenses at 10 times the rate of Whites." This is a racial disparity that has come from racist stereotypes and the enslavement of one man that started an evolving institution of free labor.

One does not have to speculate about what a black female slave's life was like; she was mistreated in almost every way imaginable, including abuse by fellow white women. One Virginia slave, Elizabeth Sparks recounts her **Aunt Caroline's experience** saying,

> "Mistress Miller, she used to make my Aunt Caroline knit all day. And when she get so tired after dark that she get sleepy she make her stand up and knit. Mistress would work her so hard that she'd go to sleep standing up. **And every time her head nod or her knees sag, that lady come upon her head with a switch. That's the way white folks was. Some had gizzards instead of hearts.**" (Unchained Memories: Readings from the Slave Narratives, bold emphasis added)

Aunt Caroline's experience, of working for insurmountable hours was not uncommon to slaves. In addition to this type of treatment, she was expected to endure through the demotion of her humanness, the emotional duress

WOMEN'S RIGHTS DURING SLAVERY

Regardless of race married women were restricted in many areas including: owning finance, and owning property. All women were restricted in education and employment. Although there was a battle for women's rights in the 1800s, true progression did not realize its heights until the 1960s.

of seeing her children sold, her husband beat and whipped, not to mention the constant threat of her own scourging or potential rape.

Can you imagine what women like Aunt Caroline lived through on a daily basis? This must have been a dramatic fear-based lifestyle, always wondering what the next terror-stricken day would hold. Yet these women were able to endure through unthinkable heartache.

Not only did they fear mistreatment, but rape was also commonplace. The laws we have today were not instituted for slave women; therefore, they were always at threat, even when their own husbands were present. For example, "The feminist movement in the United States has brought about several significant reforms to the manner in which rape is defined and prosecuted in the United States. Beginning in the 1970s, the feminist anti-rape movement successfully advocated for rape shield laws and laws abolishing marital rape…"[11]

But in slavery days saying "No" would oftentimes make matters so bad that women would consent to rape freely—right in front of their husbands. It is not enough to simply hear this information in our intellect without feeling the emotional pain of both husband and wife in such a situation. The rape of black women was intentionally committed "to humiliate their husbands and undermine the integrity of slave families." (Unchained Memories: Readings from the Slave Narratives) This is how common rape was, according to the account of Reverend Ishrael Massie of Virginia,

"Lord, child, that was common. Masters and overseers used

---

[11] http://www.impowr.org/content/law-reform-efforts-rape-and-sexual-assault-united-states-america

Figure 9 Three White Men and a Black Woman (1632) by Christiaen van Couwenbergh

to make slaves that was with their husbands get up and do as they say. I've seen husbands out on the farm milking cows or cutting wood then he gets in bed with the slave himself. Some womens would fight and tussel. Others would be humbled, feared and beaten. And they told their husband…" (Unchained Memories: Readings from the Slave Narratives)

If a woman resisted rape, there was the potential of her not only being punished but being killed as Fannie Berry of Virginia accounted, "And sometimes if you rebelled the overseer would kill you. Us colored women had to go through plenty, I tell you." (Unchained Memories: Reading from the Slave Narratives)

One day a real life example of this was highlighted to me, while talking to a friend about modern-day adoption. My friend was a white woman who had four of her own children and adopted an African baby girl. We began to talk about her experience raising a black baby girl and people's reactions. She then shared about one of her friends, a black woman, married to a white man. This woman adopted children of multiple ethnicities. *When I asked about people's responses to the black woman's choice to adopt ethnicities different*

ARE YOU A NANNY?

When one black woman chose to adopt different ethnicities from her own, she shared that people would stop her, asking, "Are you a nanny?" Sometimes questions reveal deeper rooted mentalities that we otherwise would not admit nor see. If this was a white woman with her black children such questions would not be asked, but because of our history-black women were nannies to white women's children even many years post slavery, while being forced to neglect their own children—there is an underlining assumption that this is a black women's role. To serve and help. How dare you parent our children? *But it is okay if we help your poor children...appears to be the double standard.*

---

from her own, she shared that people would stop her asking if she was a nanny.

This is one of many illustrations highlighting deeply entrenched mentalities we have regarding a black woman's role as servant. She must stay in that role in our minds, until we intentionally choose to give her a higher honor. If we choose not to, there is a default prejudice at play resulting from years of slavery in our nation.

Not only were black women seen as servants, created to produce more children for their masters, but their rights as mothers were also removed. Another well-known abolitionist, Frederick Douglass recalled his experience regarding his biological mother saying,

> **"I do not recollect of ever seeing my mother by the light of day. She was with me in the night.** She would lie down with me, and get me to sleep, but long before I waked she was gone. Very little communication ever took place between us. Death soon ended what little we could have while she lived, and with it her hardships and suffering. She died when I was about seven years old, on one of my master's farms, near Lee's Mill. I was not allowed to be present during her illness, at her death, or burial. She was gone long before I knew anything about it. Never having enjoyed, to any considerable extent, her soothing presence, her tender and watchful care, I received the tidings of her death with much the same emotions I

EXCERPT FROM WHAT ADOPTING A WHITE GIRL TAUGHT ONE BLACK FAMILY

By Tony Dokoupil, Newsweek 4.22.2009

Several pairs of eyes follow the girl as she pedals around the playground in an affluent suburb of Baltimore. But it isn't the redheaded fourth grader who seems to have moms and dads of the jungle gym nervous on this recent Saturday morning. It's the African-American man—six feet tall, bearded and wearing a gray hooded sweatshirt—watching the girl's every move. Approaching from behind, he grabs the back of her bicycle seat as she wobbles to a stop. "Nice riding," he says, as the fair-skinned girl turns to him, beaming. "Thanks, Daddy," she replies. The onlookers are clearly flummoxed.

As a black father and adopted white daughter, Mark Riding and Katie O'Dea-Smith are a sight at best surprising, and at worst so perplexing that people feel compelled to

should have probably felt at the death of a stranger."
(Douglass 18-19, bold added)

Frederick Douglass, the Great Abolitionist at the tender age of 18 years old

EXCERPT FROM WHAT ADOPTING A WHITE GIRL TAUGHT ONE BLACK FAMILY

By Tony Dokoupil, Newsweek 4.22.2009

respond. Like the time at a Pocono Mountains flea market when Riding scolded Katie, attracting so many sharp glares that he and his wife, Terri, 37, and also African-American, thought "we might be lynched." And the time when well-intentioned shoppers followed Mark and Katie out of the mall to make sure she wasn't being kidnapped. Or when would-be heroes come up to Katie in the cereal aisle and ask, "Are you OK?"—even though Terri is standing right there.

But the Ridings' experience runs counter to these popular notions of harmony. And adoption between races is particularly fraught.

So-called transracial adoptions have surged since 1994, when the Multiethnic Placement Act reversed decades of outright racial matching by banning discrimination against adoptive families on the basis of race. But the growth has been all one-sided. The number of white families adopting outside their race is growing and is now in the thousands, while cases like Katie's—of a black family adopting a nonblack child—remain frozen at near zero.

Is it racism? The Ridings tend to think so, and it's hard to blame them. To shadow them for a day, as I recently did, is to feel the unease, notice the negative attention and realize

EXCERPT FROM WHAT ADOPTING A WHITE GIRL TAUGHT ONE BLACK FAMILY

By Tony Dokoupil, Newsweek 4.22.2009

that the same note of fear isn't in the air when they attend to their two biological children, who are 2 and 5 years old. It's fashionable to say that the election of Barack Obama has brought the dawn of a post-racial America. In the past few months alone, The Atlantic Monthly has declared "the end of white America," The Washington Post has profiled the National Association for the Advancement of Colored People's struggle for relevance in a changing world, and National Public Radio has led discussions questioning the necessity of the annual Black History Month. Perhaps not surprising, most white and black Americans no longer cite racism as a major social problem, according to recent polls.

The separation and pain women like Frederick Douglass" mother must have experienced is both unnatural and demeaning, taking away their GOD given role as caregiver. This is one of many glimpses into a slave woman's life.

In conclusion, we can determine that the treatment of women in general during that time-period was devastating, but the treatment of black women was beyond degradation.

The mentalities were also strikingly twisted and the fact that well respected, Christian white men shared their female slaves with their sons is even more sickening (perhaps a root to many lust strongholds in our boys today) (McLaurin 26-27). This explains the uprising of sexual immorality that would explode in America in days to come. Imagine the feelings of the wives and daughters of these men. But unfortunately, the white wives and daughters may have typically saw it as the slave woman's fault. They were taught black slave women were Jezebels, responsible for deceitfully seducing their men.

QUESTION FOR MEDITATION: What is your subconscious view of black women? Pray and ask GOD to show you if you have an oversexualized or servant-slave view of black women. Then ask Him for His perspective. If necessary, humbly ask for forgiveness and a change of mentality in this area of your heart. 1 John 1:9 says God is faithful and just to forgive and cleanse you of all unrighteousness.

SEXUAL REVOLUTION

Could Slavery have been America's first sexual revolution, an underground sexual institution? Today we find sexual images in the grocery store, on billboard ads, and on commercials. 40 million American people regularly visit porn sites. Confessing our past may help heal our current problem.

THE TREATMENT OF MEN: MY MASTER STOLE MY FATHER ROLE

Understanding the treatment of men during slavery can help us understand the potential origins of black fatherlessness rates, and marital rates in black America. Not only were women oppressed by the system of slavery, but men were also stripped of their dignity and manhood. As a married woman, I am well-aware of how important the role of men in our society is and I know that men have innate desires for respect. They have a natural care for their wives, desiring to protect and provide. When this is taken away, it is one of the most painful experiences a man can undergo.

Figure 10 Homes all across the south, like this South Carolina Plantation Slave Home, were filled with pain as fathers were ripped from their rightful protector role

This is exactly what happened through slavery. Men, alike women and children, were considered chattel property. Therefore, they had no rights to marriage, family, fatherhood, possessions nor any other necessity. They were forced to watch their mothers, wives and daughters suffer through abuse. They could not fight back without the threat of harm to their lives or their loved ones. And

117

they were made to be reminded of this repeatedly to ensure they did not usurp the forced authority of slave owners..

Even free men were not exempt from the chilling grip of serfdom. Instead, they were always in danger of being abducted, as in Solomon Northrup's unique story. Solomon was a free man his entire life when suddenly his "normality" would change into a horror story. He wrote the book, *Twelve Years a Slave,* Narrative of Solomon Northrup, a Citizen of New York, Kidnapped in Washington City in 1841, and Rescued in 1853, from a Cotton Plantation Near the Red River in Louisiana. This slave narrative sheds incredible light onto the unfair structure of slavery. But it also gives insight into the cloud of fear all blacks must have been living under during that time, men included. Frederick Douglass shared some of this emotion when speaking of Solomon Northrup saying,

"Think of it: For thirty years a man, with all a man's hopes, fears and aspirations—with a wife and children to call him by the endearing names of husband and father—with a home, humble it may be, but still a home…then for twelve years a thing, a chattel personal, classed with mules and horses. …Oh! It is horrible. It chills the blood to think that such are." (Northrup ix)

Solomon Northrup did not go through an intangible historical institution. This was real, he came out by the grace of GOD. Solomon was a real man, living in this same nation we now travel through so freely. But Solomon could not travel without the threats of his extinction. And he lost it all- his wife, his children, his home, to become what Frederick Douglass mournfully described as, "A thing."

He grieved two major roles in this process, **husband and father.** These two roles are still lost in the households of the black community.

Solomon Northrup proved to us all that it is possible to be "educated, curious, and…fully aware of (one's) former freedom and dignity" yet still remain a slave (Northrup x-xi). This was not a result of Solomon's poor choices, nor a lack of his ability to be an upstanding citizen. It was due to the mishandling of freedom in Southern white plantations.

Solomon also proved that the concept of being less than a man due to the color of one's skin was absurb, for he was already operating as a competent, valuable father and husband. Rather, slavery had all to do with a misconstrued concept in people's minds, a stronghold of the mind that needed to be deconstructed. The same remains true in our day. Furthermore, the black male was no longer the head of the household or the "dominant" leader, instead he was less than human.

BUT HE'S A THUG!

I remember watching the 2015 Baltimore riots scroll across my hotel screen as a white commentator blurted out these young black men were "thugs." My heart dropped. The bias is not that no blacks are criminals but it is biased to treat white young criminals as only troubled youth, deserving a life.

Dr. Joy DeGruy Leary, one of the foremost experts on generational trauma in the black community, describes this stolen fatherhood role sharing,

> "In most families the dominant male is the father. Who was the dominant male in a slave's life? The master was figuratively, if not literally, the father. It was the master who more often than not became the imprint for male parental behavior…and this imprint was passed on through generations. At its foundation, this imprint was dominated by the necessity to control others through violence and aggression." (Leary 123)

When a man's role is perverted in this way, or completely removed in many cases, all that is left to fall back on is the main male figure, in this case it was slave masters. Women and children had to learn what fatherhood and the husband/romantic role was from this derogatory example. It has had devastating effects on post slavery generations. These views of manhood have grossly effected how our boys and men see themselves and women. But it has also, oftentimes unknowingly affected how the white community tends to see black men in America.

Slave men were not even given the rights to be cared for by their children or wives at an elderly age. Sojourner Truth's father is an excellent example of this loss. He died in a very shameful, suffering way, due to neglect and extreme poverty. After losing his wife, blinded and barely able to care for his self, he was finally freed. His owner needed to loose another liability. Then his two elderly friends, sent with him to a wooded cabin, died. He was finally left alone, unable to do basic tasks like taking baths. His children could not tend to him because they themselves were slaves. (Truth 17)

Sojourner Truth's father's experience can be analogized to the tense feelings currently heating America's thermometer. The disillusionment and frustration of being told "you are free" while being ill-equipped with the resources to enjoy that freedom fully is many times unrecognized by middle class white America. These two worlds must find both historical and contemporary understanding for us to move forward.

One tobacco worker, when asked what life was like for a tobacco slave in the nineteenth century, exclaimed, "We were awakened by the blowing of a horn before sunrise by the overseer... worked all day to sundown. Bout time to go...to dinner, you carried a little dinner with you...slaves were driven top speed and whipped at the snap of

HONORING BLACK MEN

For years the black male was not respected as the head of his household. Even after slavery's close, black men were made to look down when in a white man's presence and were not respected. This has caused a lot of shame and disrespect. It is vital we Break the Trends by honoring our men as worthy in our words, tonality and assumptions. We can give the gift of Honor.

a finger by the overseer. We had four overseers on the farm, all hired white men. **I've seen men beaten until they dropped in their traps or by their clubs. Women, stripped down to their waist and cowhided.**" (*Up from Slavery* DVD, Bold Emphasis Added)

These men were beaten until they could no longer stand. And these were not weak men. They conducted manual labor sunup to sundown. They survived the Middle Passage and worked in extreme weather conditions with limited food. They were our Heroic Survivors. Their backs literally built the United States of America. Yet they were treated as if they were inhuman. Their spirit was not broken but the traumatic effects of being beat in front of their own women and children have lingered. And even worse, they were unable to protect their women, watching them "stripped down to their waist," in utter exposure to be "cowhided."

The magnitude of this type of

SLAVES OUR HEROES?

Recently there was a racial debate on Facebook about whether "normal Americans" could be heroes but who we deem heroic is subject our values. Slaves were heroic because of their contribution to America through insurmountable adversity, their deep faith and character. Their example of sacrifice, hope and forgiveness is something we as Americans can hold onto as praiseworthy.

treatment must hit more than our minds, it must hit our souls, our emotions. We must feel the impact of this great atrocity before we can deeply care about the rooted injustices of the African American community- right in our own beloved nation.

We must feel the impact of this great atrocity, Slavery, before we can deeply care about the rooted injustices of the African American community- right in our own beloved nation. But how can we feel unless we first know the storyline?

These men also experienced the humiliation of being sold or their children snatched from their arms at slave auctions, "Talk about something awful, the slave owners was shouting and selling chillun' to one man and the momma and pappy to another." (Unchained Memories) This had to be the epitome of cruelty. The shrieking sound of children, mothers and fathers helplessly screaming out to one another as they knew they would never see their own family members again; this was a death experience. Just as we would go to an auction today to purchase an item, an object, these men were sold for a price. But there were also times they powerfully reflected their inward strength as a former slave, Robert Falls of Tennessee proclaimed,

> "If I had my life to live over I would die fighting rather than be a slave again. I want no man's yoke on my shoulders no more. Now my father, he was a fighter. He was as mean as a bear. He was so bad to fight and so troublesome he was sold four times to..maybe a heap more times." (Unchained Memories)

These are only a few glimpses into the mistreatment towards our black men. Perhaps these accounts have begun to cause you to reflect on your own life experience as a black man, a black woman, a white man, a white woman or even someone of another ethnicity.

QUESTION FOR MEDITATION: Have you realized that you have taken on generational or societal misconceptions towards black men? Do you tend to blame black men for the issues in society or see them as a problem? Do you have a negative perspective of yourself or your own community (if you are a black American)?

Take a moment to write down examples of mentalities in your life or racist experiences you have downplayed towards black men. Pray asking GOD to forgive you for these perspectives, whether they were known or unknown. Then receive a new view through the understanding obtained in this chapter.

THE TREATMENT OF CHILDREN

What happened to children? Like the precious ones born to the beautiful mulatto slave, Eliza? A man named Solomon Northrup met her in the most saddened way, at a 'slave pen,' called Williams Slave Pen of Washington D.C. People would walk by this pen daily, unaware of the depth of evil behind its walls.

These children had to see, hear
and experience other agonizing and inappropriate
(for lack of better terms) happenings.
Most of which, we would never
allow our own children to
even view on a movie screen.

There Northrup found well-cultured Eliza huddled up with her children, travailing in pain. She was to be separated from her babies and Northrup described her as "throwing herself upon the floor, and encircling the children in her arms" (Northrup 30-31).

He continued sharing, "Soon they would have no mother to comfort them—they would be taken from her" and this was the experience of many black children of her day.

One can only wonder what these children must have felt the day they were deceitfully snatched from their mother to be sold. The many nightmares they must have endured in a "pen," the years of longing for their mother's touch, the wonderment of what the fate of their mother would be, the memories of their mothers screaking cries, and the gentle feeling of her hands between their well-kept strands of hair...Because of this institution, these memories, however fond or demeaning, would be the only connection to their parents, even into adulthood.

These children had to see, hear and experience other agonizing and inappropriate (for lack of better terms) happenings. Most of which, we would never allow our own children to even

BLACK FOSTER CARE

Today's black children are behind new walls, the walls of Foster Care. Black children are twice as likely than white children to be taken from parent's homes. Furthermore, 26% of foster care children are black, which is double the U.S. black child population. Could this trend have begun in slavery?

view on a movie screen. For example, Frederick Douglass and many others had to see horrifying actions and images as a child.

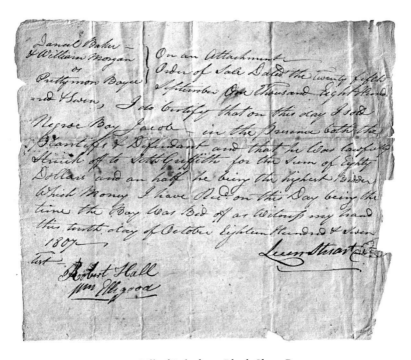

Figure 11 1807 Auction Bill of Sale for a Black Slave Boy.

He saw his aunt, naked, which alone is unacceptable, he saw her devalued to a sexual figure, to be beaten by the master.

What does this do to the mind of a young child? Our children saw act after act. They never received counseling. They were traumatized. They then had to raise the next generation, while in survival mode. How do we overcome this state of trauma as a people and a nation? It is unquestionable that this has generated the national crisis we are facing today.

These family splits and inappropriate experiences created the generational divides we see in chocolate cities today. They have also created a lack of emotional connectivity to one's self and others. A generation of orphans was birthed as these children were split from their mothers on the auction block (Douglass 18).

Our children saw act after act. They
never received counseling. They were
traumatized. They had to raise the next
generation, while in survival mode.
How do we overcome this state of
trauma as a people and a nation?
It is absurd to believe this has not
generated the national crisis
we are facing today.

These children were treated in ways that would put criminals behind bars forever in our day. One child, horrendously taken into the hands of cruel slave masters, was placed under so much fear that when seeing his own mother, he lied saying she was not his mom. The poor baby was terrified of his captors. When finally returned to her, she described her "examination" of her sweet son in utter shock,

> "She commenced as soon as practicable to examine the boy, and found, to her utter astonishment, that from the crown of his head to the sole of his foot, the callosities and indurations on his entire body were most frightful to behold. His back she described as being like her fingers, as she laid them side by side." (Truth 36-37, emphasis added)

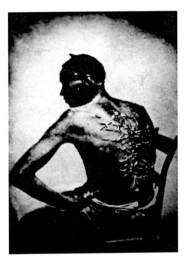

Figure 12 This image of Peter, a Louisiana abused black slave expresses the common mistreatment of even slave children. Taken April 1836 then shared by abolitionist in later years.

The mother sharing this account was Sojourner Truth, a heroine, the great heroine, slave abolitionist and preacher. Her son had to see the unimaginable, telling his mother, **"Oh, this is nothing, mammy—if you should see Phillis, I guess you'd scare! She had a little baby, and Fowler cut her till the milk as well as blood ran down her body."** (Truth 36-37)

He was describing the imagery of a woman who's breast were still full of milk. They cut her breasts until milk and blood ran down her sides. The place of provision became pain. This is the extent of inhumane treatment slave children had to witness. If we can empathize with the mistreatment of Jews who have survived the holocaust, our hearts must bleed and grieve over the millions of slaves who endured this type of treatment for hundreds of years' time. We can no longer turn a blind eye because it is uncomfortable.

Figure 13 This pig trough was on display with 1700 and 1800 buildings in Kentucky. Slave children were made to eat out of troughs under the house like pigs.

The abuse didn't end there. Children were even fed in troughs like pigs. One slave, Octavia George accounted,

"I remember quite well how those…children used to have to eat. They were fed in boxes and troughs under the house. They were fed corn meal mush and beans. When this was poured into their boxes they would gather around it, same as we see pigs, horses, cattle gather around troughs today." (Unchained Memories DVD)

This was of course no way for a child to be treated nor fed, but this is what our children had to endure, seeing animals eat out of the same containers as they were made to eat. That alone must have echoed the lie in their hearts that they were equivalent to the value of a pig, a horse, a dog.

They were uneducated because it was illegal for children to go to school or learn to read or write. They were owned by other children as Texas slave, Francis Black, recalls being told by a white boy named Jimmy, 'Come on nigger, let's ride around the farm.' Francis replied, 'I ain't no nigger.' Jimmy then told him, 'Yes you is, my paw paid $200 for you, he bought you for to play with me.' (Unchained Memories DVD) Apparently from accounts like Francis', these white parents would "buy" black children for their children to play with; traces of this can be seen in our day.

I remember times of not being invited to play with the white children, or go to their sleepovers because of my skin complexion. But all the lighter skin black girls were invited to go. It is hard for some to believe, but these behaviors have been deeply entrenched in our children's hearts.

Children, during slavery days, were made to fan flies off white families throughout dinner times. *They quickly became human fly swatters; their humanity became the source to the upscale lifestyle of their southern slave masters.*

Finally, as we reflect upon these children's demise, I will leave you with the words of Texan, James Green:

"I never knowed my age 'till after the war when master got out a big book and it shows I'm 25 year old, shows I was 12 when I was brought and 800 dollars paid for me...Long came a Friday and that an unlucky star day and I playing around the house and Williams come up and say...will you...walk down the street with me? My mammy say, 'Alright Jim, you be a good boy.' That the last iem I ever heard her speak or ever see her." (Unchained Memories)

EMPATHY OR SYMPATHY

There has been a problem with the black community being seen as a "needy" people that we are to help but there has been a lack of True Empathy (Sharing in the Feelings of another's heart). As one begins <u>to feel her pain</u>, true love develops no longer feeling sorry for her in pity, but coming alongside her in heartfelt friendship.

QUESTION FOR MEDITATION: If you have children, you can relate to the desire to see them healthy, happy and whole. Even if you do not have children, the events described are deeply moving. Take time to reflect upon what was done to these children. Begin to pray for the healing of the white and black communities, both have been affected by these happenings in our nation's roots. Ask GOD to give you a compassionate heart, compassion towards a community that has been generationally mistreated and wounded due to such atrocities.

THE PROBLEM WITH SYMPATHY

At first sight sympathy may sound or look good but so often white missionaries and philanthropists have reached out to us, frustrated with the lack of progress they have made in connecting with the black community. Usually, on a heart level the problem has come from a lack of trust between the two parties- when people feel you are coming to "help them" instead of know and love them, they become disheartened and feel less than you. But when you get to know them through a ministry of presence, love, care, feeling their pain with them, you are more easily received. *Have you been carrying a sympathetic or empathetic feeling towards blacks?* No more feeling sorry is needed. It is time to feel with her and see her strength. That is, if we want to see true unity.

Chapter 5
Emancipate Us

We can do this. Our history is full of overcoming, waking up, against the odds and in the dark. It only takes a few strong people who are willing to be Heroes.

SOME WERE ENLISTED...OTHERS LED

The Abolitionist Movement, a genius collage of poets, speakers, journalists, everyday heroes, feminists, soldiers, and politicians, was the precursor to the greatest war in American history. Men and women, black and white, were guided into this occasion wearing all sorts of ensembles—some were found donning military apparel, others freshly worn ex-slave rags, while some even wore the finest tea gowns of their day. But they all came strolling in with pride, a sense of historical significance and a determination to liberate the souls and frames of the ebony toned forced workers.

We are forever indebted to these courageous figures whose countenances, however varied, have become one breathtaking masterpiece etched in the benchmark of time. This collage of moving characters, ready to embark on a journey together, escalating into a common narrative and marching into the reception of history, while clothed in varying adornment, all capture the essence of how we attained this formidable singularity as a people called American. Without these greatest of performers, we would likely have experienced an even direr magnitude of racial pain, yet evolving into inevitable freedom—at least that of the physical type.

What upon earth is a matter with the
American people? Do they really covet the
world's ridicule as well as their own social
and political ruin? The national edifice is on
fire. Every man who can carry a bucket of
water or remove a brick is wanted. Yet
government leaders persistently refuse to
receive as soldiers the slaves the very class of
men which has a deeper interest in the defeat
and humiliation of the rebels than all others.
Such is the pride, the stupid prejudice and
folly that rules the hour.

Frederick Douglass

In the following pages, you will find the stories of these distinguished leaders. Most of this discussion will focus on the lives and achievements of already well-known revolutionaries such as Frederick Douglass, William Lloyd Garrison and Sojourner Truth.

Views of Blacks, Slavery	Views of Blacks Today
Blacks are...	**Blacks are...**
Intemperate	Intemperate
Ignorant	Angry
Lazy	Lazy
Thieves	Thieves
Other Common Views...	**Other Common Views...**
White are Suffering Too	Whites are Suffering too
Efforts Can't Improve Them, It's their Choices	Efforts Can't Improve Them, It's their Choices
They Should Achieve More	They Should Achieve More
Whites are their Missionaries	Whites are their Missionaries
They Should go Save Africa	They Should Go Do Missions

Figure 14 While many argue that we are not in slavery days, the same views many white Americans had of blacks during slavery continue today. Time has helped but has not eliminated these subconscious beliefs in some white Americans.

This is not at all to be redundant, rather to expound upon the history from a lesser taught perspective, that of an African American woman living in the 21st century. As a descendant of an abolitionist heroine, I am humbly submitting my commentary into the many historical documents already eloquently telling the abolitionist storyline. I believe you will find this a very interesting perspective especially when considering the lack of African American storytelling in our current public school systems.

It would do us all good to gain a deeper understanding of these personages from an angle that may in fact be nearer their original vantage points. Some were enlisted, others led, then there were those who created a tumultuous uproar as they entered the Movement. …It was the sound of a ready writer, a spirited journalist, a quick-witted novelist, a longing soldier, and an imaginative poet. It was the words of a well-learned orator and an illiterate ex-slave. It was the actions of aggressive activists, unwilling to take gradual emancipation for an answer. These sounds, words and actions became the impressive bright sparks that would light the embers of the American Civil War.

OUR NEED FOR ABOLITION

It is incredible how transferrable the views of northern whites during slavery are to current Americans. Listen to these words that summarize the views of white colonizers at of the

BENEATH THE SURFACE

Many times we can benefit from seeing people beyond their actions. I used to see their behaviors and miss their need. But asking the question, "What pain needs to be healed?" has really helped me get to the heart of the situation. Beneath anger, ignorance, intemperance, and laziness is one culprit: Pain.

great abolitionist, William Lloyd Garrison's day,

> "colonization orators tells us that the free blacks are pests in the community; **that they are an intemperate, ignorant, lazy, thievish class**; that their condition is worse than that of the slaves; and that no efforts to improve them in this country can be successful…in the next breath we are told what might works these miserable outcasts are to achieve—that they are missionaries of salvation, who are to illumine all Africa" (Davis 191, emphasis added).

These words bring us into the **heart** of the people's message. It is easy to see falsehoods and rooted, biased mentalities in this perspective. These perspectives are also due to a lack of education. They continue today. I recently went to a bank and encountered systemic poverty. It was in a location where blacks may be viewed similarly: intemperate, ignorant, lazy and thievish. In fact, I saw what looked like grand intemperance as a twenty-something black girl, began to "go crazy" at her steering wheel. She was literally flinging her head back and forth, throwing her hands up in display of utter frustration.

As I watched her and others going in and out of the bank, more displays of misplaced turmoil became evident. After her traumatic moment, the young lady regained her composure, pushed her foot on the gas pedal, drove into reverse and exited the bank. My heart began to wonder, why didn't I go help her. *But it was too late.* I continued to bemoan the injustices done to the black community, as my husband sat quietly listening.

But it wasn't over.

There was more. I see a black "family" walk out the back, walking towards either their car or "the projects" (government housing) across the street. The mother begins to curse at her child…more pent up emotion fumes out of her heart. But that day I did not see *intemperate, ignorant, lazy and thievish people*. Instead, overwhelmingly, tears filled my eyes as I saw the streamlined connection—generations of locked up expression, their actions expressed the exact words I was preaching at my one-man congregation, my husband.

That day I was looking at systematic, generational poverty, ironically sitting at a bank. Simultaneously, images of the predominantly white congregation I shared with recently flashed before me; my heart beat with grief. They did not understand our plight. They may have had sympathy (feeling bad for our people) but

CONTRADICTORY THINKING

In one breath blacks were held to be impossibly horrid and untamable; in the next breath, they needed to change and achieve. This same mentality has continued in our day. Sometimes it is unintentional, yet it is still contradictory. Do we realize that holding the black community to such a high standard while considering them untamable is having high expectations while underestimating her ability? It is time we elevate our viewpoint of her potential while remembering that painful discrimination can oftentimes hinder the most promising of individuals.

many did not place themselves on equal playing ground.

Did they ask the vital questions, *How would I feel? What would my life be like if I was a black man living in America?* If these questions were asked, they would move more quickly from the sympathetic, *Oh I feel so sorry for you and I'm here to help you because I know I'm better than you deep down in my heart* to the empathetic, *I would be a mess too if I ever had to bounce back from hundreds of years of oppression so let's go on a journey together.*

The fact is, we cannot have reconciliation meetings that actually work when we do not FEEL the pain of the black community, when we do not KNOW the extent of pain blacks feel, when we do not take FULL ownership of our own heart. The injustice rolls on and we must call ourselves to full responsibility if we are ever going to see change.

We must weep not out of pity nor feeling sorry for the poor black folks in pain. We must weep out of the compassion we would feel if we were in their shoes, as fellow humans. We must understand the historical context and that in many ways, today's culture is the same as years bygone, especially if your skin is black.

That was Garrison's point. How can we expect blacks to be heroic, defy the odds of years of oppression, overcome systematic setbacks, be better educated, and operate at the same financial levels, yet consider them less capable? That is severely contradictory. Whether we want to admit it or not slavery has "dismal and depressing effects" due to "generations of profound discrimination." (Davis 191)

This is not an excuse, it is a matter of fact. Garrison understood the truth that **whenever we fail to examine the reason behind the constant issues, shifting blame back onto blacks, we become negligent to see our own severe misconceptions as white Americans.**

BIRTHING A VOICE: FREDERICK DOUGLASS

Shifting our current misconceptions of Black America begins with educating ourselves on the black heroes and heroines whose stories are either not fully known or not shared enough. This chapter will delve into the lives of such men and women.

> ### LET'S GO ON A JOURNEY TOGETHER
>
> Recent Pew Research article, *On Views of Race and Inequality, Blacks and Whites are Worlds Apart*, reveals that "about four-in-ten blacks are doubtful that the U.S. will ever achieve racial equality." And while 38% of whites believe "Our country has made the changes needed to give blacks equal rights with whites" only 8% of blacks believe we have come as far. Living in the suburbs, I could drive by the "hood," see it on t.v. and feel bad but I didn't know what it was like until I lived with the people in their poverty. The United States has avoided this elephant in the room for many years, including in the educational system. I didn't know how bad it was until I listened to cry of the people; I had to place some trust in their story. It's time for this to happen in America.

Allow me to introduce to you our first character, Mr. Frederick Augustus Washington Bailey, also known as Frederick Douglass. Imagine with me a man so eloquent in speech others could not believe he was ever a slave laboring in the south's peculiar institution.

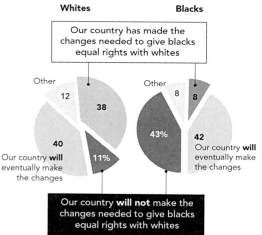

Many blacks are skeptical that the country will eventually make the changes necessary for racial equality

% saying...

Note: Whites and blacks include only non-Hispanics. Figures combine results from two questions. The first asked whether or not our country has made the changes needed to give blacks equal rights with whites; the second asked those who said the U.S. had not made the necessary changes if those changes would eventually be made or not. "Other" includes voluntary responses of "Both" or "Neither" in the first question and "Don't know/Refused" in either question. Figures may not add to 100% due to rounding.
Source: Survey of U.S. adults conducted Feb. 29–May 8, 2016. Q6F2, Q6aF2.
"On Views of Race and Inequality, Blacks and Whites are Worlds Apart"

PEW RESEARCH CENTER

Figure 15 It is clear that America's viewpoint is just as divided then as it was during slavery and the Civil Rights Movement. Whites and blacks see our nation from a different perspective. It is hard to know how bad a situation is unless you are in the victim's shoes.

This strapping young man was shoved into the common practice of "hiring out" a slave, with the intentions of "break(ing) his will". This would only backfire on his owner, Hugh Auld, as Douglass developed an even greater resistance to the institution of slavery. More than ever, he would now know first-hand the "meaning of dehumanization and the slave's longing for freedom." (Davis 229)

Whether we want to admit it or not slavery has "dismal and depressing effects" due to "generations of profound discrimination."

His escape is quite the story as Douglass was able to pass as a freed black sailor, using another "seaman's papers":

"For Douglass the traumatic moment came when, disguised as a sailor, he explained to the train conductor that as a sailor he never carried his free papers but offered his seaman's papers as a substitute. The conductor paused, but said "all right," enabling Douglass to pay his fare. There were other close calls, but Douglass finally found himself in New York, "gazing upon the dazzling wonders of Broadway." "A free state around me, and a free earth under my feet!" Suddenly, he "was a FREEMAN." (Davis 230)

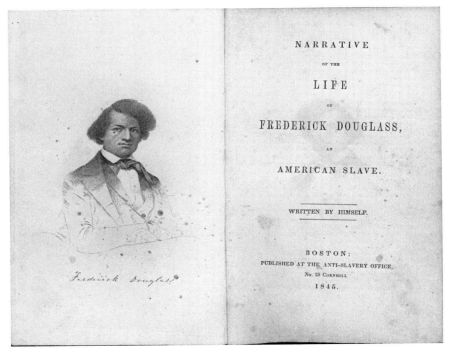

Figure 16 Douglass wrote his book The Narrative of the Life of Frederick Douglass in the year 1845 to prove that he was really a former slave. This book expounded upon his life as a slave and catapulted him into worldwide fame.

But now that Douglass was a FREEMAN, what would he do? Much like his recently freed contemporaries, it would soon settle that although he was considered a human for the first time in his life, he did not have the needed essentials to live as a human. He "wandered" for a while but with the help of the free black community would soon find his way.

Approximately six months following Douglass' escape to freedom on September 3, 1838, he would find himself in a church speaking "against colonizing blacks in Africa." (Davis 245) These seeds were planted in Douglass' heart as a young slave and Douglass was about to be "led" into one of the most significant movements in American history.

Douglass reached the minds and heart of white people more effectively than any other man of his race. James McPherson

This is how it started:

"The great event that transformed Douglass's life and launched him as the first fugitive slave to become a major orator occurred in Nantucket in August 1841. The Massachusetts Anti-Slavery Society had planned a great midsummer meeting on this lovely island, a center of Quaker-led abolitionism. It was William C. Coffin, a New Bedford Quaker bookkeeper with strong family connections in Nantucket, who urged Douglass to attend. **When Coffin spotted Douglass in the Nantucket throng, he invited** the escaped slave to stand up and speak, if so moved, according to the Quaker tradition. With considerable anxiety, Douglass chose to do so, and gave an account of his life as a slave. The huge, mostly white audience, including stellar figures such as **Garrison, Wendell Phillips, and Samuel J. May, was spellbound.** In response, Garrison rose to exclaim: "Have we been listening to a thing, a chattel personal, or a man?" The audience shouted, "A man! a man!" As Garrison continued, "Shall such a man ever be sent back to bondage from the free soil of old Massachusetts?" Now the audience rose and shouted, "No! No! No!"... "it was clear that a powerful new voice had been raised, one that demonstrated how high a former slave could stretch in a demonstration of his humanity." (Davis 231-232, bold added)

"SEND THEM BACK"

Right after slavery, there was a racist agenda to send now seemingly useless blacks back to Africa. But the freed black community did not buy into this rhetoric. Their concept was, "We built this nation with our blood, sweat and tears. We will not be sent away." This became a major focus of abolitionists.

Figure 17 Frederick Douglass founded his 13 year journal, The North Star, in the year 1847. This journal impacted the hearts of over 3,000 blacks and whites and was published monthly. (Berry and Blassingame 63)

THE ABOLITIONIST GENERAL: WILLIAM LLOYD GARRISON

The bold man, rising up with the exclamation, "Have we been listening to a thing, a chattel personal, or a man?' is William Lloyd Garrison, arguably the most influential white abolitionist in the movement. But Garrison was different. He varied in his views from previous white leaders. He began to join the sentiments of blacks who believed in **immediate abolitionism.** He was unapologetic and considered an extremist due to his direct demands. Garrison somehow seemed to have the capacity to take on the pains, feelings, and desires of the black community. He was not afraid to be mocked or to stand for the oppressed. He was a true friend to the African American people.

It is important to note that Pro-Colonization organizations like the American Colonization Society (ACS), were a mighty force in driving racist thought patterns into mainstream whites at the time. They believed blacks were going to cause trouble to America and in response developed the solution of eradicating the States of all free blacks:

"The land we have watered with our tears
and our blood is now OUR
MOTHER COUNTRY."
Richard Allen, Black Abolitionist

"Your colored population can never be rendered serviceable, intelligent or loyal; they will only, and always, serve to increase your taxes, crowd your poor-houses and penitentiaries, and corrupt an impoverish society!" (Davis 190)

But Garrison would see past this racist mindset as black abolitionist journals such as Cornish and *Walker's Freedom's Journal* fell into his young hands. It was said that he "came hungry and angry and in need of his own liberation as he learned about the desperation of millions that had been caused by slavery in America." (Davis 185) Garrison used the information he found as inspiration to lead his own movement against colonization and slavery.

In the year 1831, he founded a journal entitled *The Liberator,* which "published an all-out attack on colonization in 1832." Garrison also "founded the New-England Anti-Slavery Society in 1832, and cofounded the American Anti-Slavery Society in 1833." (Davis 185) His posture against colonization is what made him a stand-out amongst his white peers. Garrison was not the type to back down to resistance. His *Liberator* became a formidable affront to southern slavery.

BLACKS ARE DANGEROUS

The mentality that African Americans are dangerous, violent and poor came from the ACS thoughts of colonization strategically pumped into the white community to develop a desire to rid America of blacks. It is important to clear our minds of such falsehoods if we want to reconcile.

A WOMAN ON A MISSION: SOJOURNER TRUTH

Like Douglass, Sojourner Truth was both an ex-slave and committed to non-violent abolition. She was born into slavery around the year 1797, with the name Belle ("Beauty"). Also like Douglass and many other slaves, she did not know her exact birthdate.

Figure 18 Sojourner Truth was one of the greatest female American abolitionist. After feeling a call to preach against slavery to white farms and churches, she obeyed her leading and won many out of racist mentaliites.

The truth is fallacies
unchecked can become trees
of injustice in unkempt hearts.
This is at the root
of American racism.

After marrying and having five children with her husband Tom, Belle made her move. She would leave all of her children, Diana, Elizabeth, Hannah, and Peter behind; but she would keep her sweet infant Sophia with her on her journey.

Unbeknownst to her, this would initiate her change; she would become "one of the first black women in the United States to win a court case" getting her son back into her joyous arms (Family Christian Bookstore 24). Unfortunately her joy turned to sorrow after losing reclaimed Peter to "the streets," then to his journey oversees. This was the final straw. She had reached the point of disappointing personal and professional "failure":

> "Belle believed that everything she had undertaken in the city had failed. She had tried to preach, but the blacks, whom she especially wanted to reach, had rejected her."
> (Family Christian Bookstore 37)

THE BLAME GAME

It can be very uncomfortable and intimidating when we begin to see fallacies in our hearts. It is much easier to find blame in the other party without taking responsibility for our own views. Until we get down to the root of prejudice in each of our minds, we will never be authentically united. Have you ever been tempted to place the weight of injustice on the black community as they have been targeted by their own government and other races? Has your image of the black race been blighted by historical mentalities and prejudices?

All of this was at the forefront of her aching soul, when God had a *different plan in mind*. He did not see Belle as a failure. Instead, he saw her as A Rising Heroine. At 46 years old, with nothing left to her name she started all over, this is when Beauty became Sojourner.

Her ministry came out of feelings of failure. She was running from her current life which seemed to end in disappointment. She began to travel sharing the gospel, with no "support from any church or denomination and with no one advising her." (Family Christian Bookstore 37) She began to share her story of slavery and freedom. She asked God for a name and heard, "Psalm 39:12 Hear my prayer, O Lord, and give ear unto my cry…for I am a stranger with thee, **and a sojourner**, as all my fathers were." Then she decided her last name would be Truth based on John 8:32, "And ye shall know the truth, and the truth shall make you free."

She would Sojourn America as a stranger, as all her fathers were, declaring Truth.

The new Sojourner would become a great abolitionist, preaching the gospel, simply going from farm to farm. Her demeanor? A tall, confident black woman. Now that was not as striking and unusual as the fact that she a woman, a black woman at that…speaking to an all-white "congregation." That was unheard of. Soon Sojourner became well known as a prominent "inspirational speaker with a stirring message." It was because of her strength and someone's request for her to "speak about her life as a slave that she was thrust into the movement." (Family Christian Bookstore 41)

The remainder was history. She added to her repertoire, Women's Right's Activist coining the phrase, "Ain't I A Woman" stirring a shocked audience with her timeless speech on women's rights. Furthering her impact, Sojourner had her autobiography written by her friend Olive Gilbert. Then she travelled with the abolitionist lecture circuit sharing her book. Truth was strongly challenged to be an abolitionist by William Lloyd Garrison and others. She grasped the hearts of listeners with her short but stunning speeches. Eventually, Sojourner would join the likes of Frederick Douglass and Harriet Beecher Stowe in the movement. In the end, she became a nationally known leader, meeting with the likes of President Lincoln. In fact, she encouraged him with the story of the Biblical figure, Daniel.

And this is the story of how a Belle became God's Sojourner, shining truth on a darkened nation.

HISTORICAL LESSONS
What Can We Learn from Garrison?

Garrison profoundly took on the heart of African American people as if he were "in their shoes." He demonstrated empathy, which is defined as "the ability to share in another's emotions, thoughts, or feelings" (Webster's Collegiate Dictionary, 4th Edition) America is in need of modern day Garrisons that can bridge gaps between races. How can imagining yourself in others "shoes" help create a bridge of empathy to someone who is a little different than you?

BUT, HAVE WE LEARNED THE LESSON?

The work of Frederick Douglass and others can be used as a foundational tool to see backwards views of the black community. There has always been a way for Americans to deny wrong viewpoints and injustices, but that does not have to continue. It is vitally important that we reconsider Douglass' thoughts in modern times. This man who "argues that as a man, he was "entitled to the rights and privileges of a man" continues to speak for the black community today. (Berry and Blassingame 58)

Have we listened to the prophetic words of our forefathers?

Men and women, both black and white, were persecuted and fought because of their determination to be treated as "men" or "women." They deserve that right, just as Black Americans deserve that right today.

OUR FOREFATHERS: ABOLITIONIST HEROES

We can do this. Our history is full of overcoming, waking up, against the odds and in the dark. It only takes a few strong people who are willing to be Heroes. That means they go against popular opinion. They choose to deny themselves. And they decide that being selfless is the answer. When this happens the true heroes win spiritual battles with Love. Our forefathers have already shown us the way. Why reinvent the wheel?

REFLECTION QUESTIONS

1. "What upon earth is a matter with the American people?" Those words ring true today. How do you think considering the emotions of others may help us find deeper levels of unity? How could you apply that principle to current relationships and interaction with other races?

2. What heart pangs have you felt reading this chapter? What may that reveal about how God may want to use you as a modern day abolitionist?

3. If you are white, what lessons can you learn from William Lloyd Garrison's bold approach to reconciliation? How could you be a voice for black friends, even in white circles? Do you face any fears that could be resolved?

4. If you are black, what lessons can you learn from Frederick Douglass and Sojourner Truth? How can you be an effective voice to your white friends, expressing the truth in love? Do you face any fears that could be resolved?

Chapter 6
Civil Wars

"I, John Brown, am now quite certain that the crimes of this guilty land can never be purged away but with blood."
John Brown, American Abolitionist

RESURRECTIONS OF INJUSTICE

This Christmas was different. But it was wonderful. We stayed a couple days after Christmas and bonded over a Christmas story—the bombing of a residential home in Philadelphia (1985) and the consequential burning of remaining neighbors' homes (50-60 houses). Well, that's not quite a Christmas story, but it is worth knowing.

I remember seeing what must have been replays of this incident on television as a child. I remember my parents discussing this tragedy. How could the city police force bomb a home housing six innocent children? Was this "civilized" racism at one of its worst forms?

In watching the 2013 documentary, "Let the Fire Burn" another angle of the story is told, the African American perspective. Voice is given to how blacks must feel when incidents like this occur. And these pop-up incidents seem to occur over and over throughout our history, compounding to a climatic moment. This Christmas, my heart swelled with that familiar feeling of shock, anger and

Figure 19 In 1985, city officials made the decision to bomb a Philadelphia home and then allow the burning of the remaining 50-60 homes housing six innocent children. When questioned, the lack of remorse and viewpoint of these black tenants revealed entrenched racist views. Regardless of their beliefs, they were humans treated as animals.

frustration so common to blacks. So many questions filled my heart. This was not the Jim Crow Era, Civil Rights Movement nor the Civil War. Slavery was far gone. *Yet all the police involved in this bombing walked away scotch free.* Because of the group's beliefs, they were put on caution. But I wondered, What if this was an all-white hippie group refusing to blend with society? What if an all-black police force bombed their home (mind you, with innocent children inside)? What would that turn out be? I do not have to wonder.

Every one of those black officers would be in jail. For life. Yet, we consider racial injustice to be a thing of the past.

Five adults and six children were killed in this bombing. My jaw dropped as I watched each police officer and the police commissioner wiggled his way out of the decision to drop the bomb. When the incident occurred, the head officer looked to his staff and coldly stated, "Let the fire

FORGIVE AND FORGET

Is expecting blacks to forgive and forget gracious? When she has to forget she is being asked to forget her history, which has already been stolen from her grip. It's too much to ask her to forget or become colorblind. Her ethnicity is something she cherishes and a part of her legacy. The joy comes with the pain.

burn."

Due to this decision, over 60 other homes were then destroyed, only to be replaced with substandard housing which had to be torn down years later. *But where is the care for the black community and her possessions? Where is the care for her babies?*

How could the city police force bomb a house with six innocent children inside? Was this "civilized" racism at one of its worst forms?

This black-led back to nature, green movement, although controversial, did not deserve such treatment. They did not deserve to lose their children's lives. And the one baby boy left to interview did not deserve to lose his mother, the closest person he knew. The women left to interview did not deserve to be questioned in a clearly biased manner, withholding sensitivity to their loss. But one of the greatest clues to how deep the heart of prejudice can go was when the police force placed "Nigger Lover" signs on the locker of the one officer who jumped to save the black boy's life as the poor baby fell from the home head first on the ground.

If this was not a racist attack then why such strong statements of hatred? Why beat one of the men mercilessly who came out of the house, hands held high in surrender? Why tell the black priest in a subsequent community interview, "You are not like them, you can't understand them."

The priest's response? "I knew every one of them by name, to me they were human beings." You could see a look of stunned awareness come onto the faces of those white officers as their viewpoint of this black "tribe" people as less than human was brought right to the surface.

And this is the problem we continue to face today. Black youth are termed thugs and criminals for the same situations white youth are deemed troubled kids. These are the types of events that lead to Civil War.

Join me in discovering how a string of similar situations in the past tore our nation to pieces. Knowing our past can help us avoid making the same mistakes today!

THE RAID THAT SPARKED THE CIVIL WAR

Although all the previous chapter's abolitionists strongly believed in the values of non-violence, the tide in views would dramatically shift in days prior to the Civil War. Eventually abolitionists began believing that only violence would bring an end to slavery's gripping hold. This was largely due to the Fugitive Slave Law, enacted in the year 1850. This law equipped Northern police officers and kidnappers to return runaway slaves to their Southern slave masters. In fact, the federal government was responsible for enforcing this law. Warning ads were sent out to give the black community notice. They had to protect themselves from police officers who did not have their best interest in mind.

Because of this legalization, more and more "moderates" began to cry out that the nation was in spiritual crisis. They began to believe that a great separation was occurring between north and south. And, "an increasing number of non resistants called for a slave uprising or predicted that the streets of Boston might "yet run with blood." (Davis 251) Now slaves could not only be caught (as established in the preceding 1793 law), but the Federal Government was fully backing this movement against African American runaways:

> "Federal commissioners could now be appointed by Circuit Courts throughout the United States, where **they could issue warrants, certificates of removal, and hold hearings. Suspected fugitives were not allowed to testify, there were no juries, and if no attorney volunteered or was hired by the defendant, only the commissioner and the claimant (the master or master's agent) could speak.** Even more alarming, the law required any citizen to become a "deputy of the law" and help in the task of apprehending fugitives. **Anyone who interfered in such apprehensions, or who assisted in fugitive, could be fined as much as $1,000 or sentenced to six months in jail.**

Finally, *commissioners were to be paid ten dollars if they returned the supposed fugitive to his or her owner,* and only five dollars if they acquitted the accused black[12] " (Davis 251)

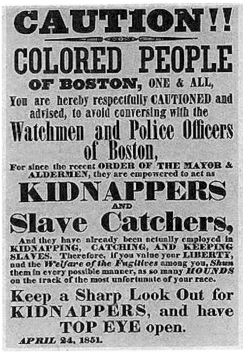

Figure 20 There is a historical backdrop of police officers taking those considered fugitive slaves, black men, women and children, back into the captivity of their slave masters. We are fighting a similar battle between law enforcement and black men today.

---

12 Injustice Continues in our Criminal Justice Systems: T*he Top 10 Most Startling Facts About People of Color and Criminal Justice in the United States,* http://americanprogress.org

In the year 1850, one U.S. dollar would have been worth $28.50; therefore anyone involved in the "assistance" of a "fugitive" slave would have been fined the equivalent of $28,450. Federal commissioners were paid with government monies to send runaway slaves back to their masters. This made America even more disjointed and emotionally charged. As seen above, "suspected fugitives were not allowed to testify, there were no juries, and if no attorney volunteered or was hired… only the commissioner or the claimant (the master or master's agent) could speak." The question became, *What is stopping any African American from being captured as a slave?*

Even the free blacks of the North were now in danger, without an opportunity to speak for themselves or testify in court. This was severe injustice. For many, this enactment justified the stance of fighting against the South—by force. In the eyes of abolitionists, there

PAID TO JAIL BLACK MEN

"What was stopping any African American from being captured as a slave?" These same feelings cross the hearts of black mothers across the U.S. Will my son be falsely accused next? 1 in every 15 black men are incarcerated while 1 in every 106 white men are jailed, creating free labor and revenue. This has become America's evolution of black slavery.

seemed to be no other way to win the battle against the black community. This blow would shake the nation to its core and the shaking would last for many years.

With the nation in a state of shocking disarray, a climatic moment was inevitable. That moment would be later termed John Brown's Raid. John Brown had a plan. He would dispossess the same federal government that had forcefully taken his people back to "Egypt" only nine years prior, by taking their weaponry. Then he would sweep these newly freed slaves up the east coast using popular Underground Railroad paths. The location he had in mind was Harper's Ferry in West Virginia.

Although Brown believed with all of his heart that the slaves would heroically rise up against their oppressors, "no slaves rose in rebellion and the local militia and resident ssurrounded the armory." Ironically, he would be "greeted" by Colonel Robert E. Lee

CLIMATIC MOMENTS

Right before the Civil War the nation began to escalate in tension. People were divided politically and racially. Current day raids and social media rants mirror tumultuous years in America's history. We can stop this from heightening with "real" conversations and comforting one another.

(later a commander in the Confederate Army) and "ton of Brown's raiders" became martyrs to some, defeated enemies to others. (Davis 254)

Although Brown did not accomplish his goal, upon the commencement of the Civil War he was memorialized a Union hero, an inspiration to soldiers who came behind his bloody trail in divergent manner. Although Brown may have seemed unsuccessful, it is widely accepted that his raid was "the single most important event, next to Lincoln's election, that drove the nation to civil war." (Gates 119) Henry Louis Gates eloquently states that this deed "convinced southerners that northerners would stop at nothing to attack their "peculiar institution," and it gave the North a heroic figure whose death, Ralph Waldo Emerson exclaimed, would "make the gallows as glorious as the cross." (Gates 119) In many ways, he accomplished more than he imagined, as his last words "written on a note handed to a guard just before his hanging" would prove to be prophetic, "I, John Brown, am now quite certain that the crimes of this guilty land can never be purged away but with blood." (http://www.history.com/topics/harpers-ferry)

Figure 21 Although John Brown's raid did not turn out successfully, it would become the catalyst igniting the American Civil War.

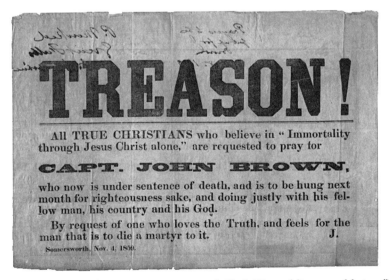

Figure 22 Although John Brown was executed Civil War soldiers would sing "John Brown's body lies a mouldering in the grave" as they descended into southern battlefields.

THE RESURRECTION OF THE SLAVE TRADE
Another factor contributing to national contention occurred at the
end of the 19th century, the resurrection of the slave trade. Although
it is unfathomable that the international slave trade (Middle Passage)
was operating that far into slavery, it is factual. This was only a few
years prior to the American Civil War. Not only that, but slaves were
being imported in large numbers. "As historian Emerson David
Fite has found, in 1859 between 35,000 and 40,000 Africans were
shipped to Havana, the world's largest slave market, for distribution
in the Americas." (Reynolds 441). This is well after the abolishing of
the slave trade in 1808, over 50 years prior.

Resurrections of Catalytic Injustice		
Date	Injustice	Outcome
1985	Philly MOVE Bombing	All Officers Non-Guilty
1999	Diallo, Unarmed, Shot 19 Times	All 4 Officers Acquitted
2014	Brown, Shot by an Officer, Ferguson, MO	Officer Wilson Acquitted
2015	Freddie Gray killed	3 Officers-Charges Dropped; 3 Acquitted
2016	Alton Sterling Shot	Officers placed on Paid Administrative Leave

Reynold's view of slavery "disappearing on its own" is also fascinating. He seemed to think that it was "far from disappearing on its own" and would have only waned away due to "industrialization and urbanization" stating, "slavery would have not made economic sense, even in the South, much beyond 1900." (Reynolds 441)

Never has this nation been so convulsed
on the subject of slavery as at the present time.
The Fugitive Slave Bill, (so called),
which has passed at the late session of
Congress, granting unlimited facilities
as it does to slave-hunters in quest of their
prey…is producing a tremendous
sensation, and rousing up all the human,
moral and religious elements in the land
against it, and against the foul system it
is designed to strengthen and protect.

William Lloyd Garrison

The climate was charged for conflict. Politicians were questioning the ability for North and South to live united or under one power. Queens began weeping over abolitionist novels. New states were formed in the west, Congress permitting them to make resolutions on the issue of legalizing slavery. This caused major eruptions specifically in the settlement of Kansas where "5,000 proslavery men invaded the territory." "Bleeding Kansas" would became the site of a 10 year bloody war (The Civil War: A Film by Ken Burns, 1990)

To make matters worse, a former slave, Dred Scott, was denied his liberation by the Supreme Court of 1857. This sparked even more divisiveness as President Lincoln stated, "As a nation we began by declaring all men are created equal. We now practically read it—All men are created equal except negroes." And "Chief Justice Roger B. Toney said a black man had no rights a white man was bound to respect." (The

HE'S NOT MY PRESIDENT

Today media is full of people saying, "Mr. Trump. He's not my president." The political divide is intense. Regardless of our views, it mirrors the feelings of many before the Civil War. Before Lincoln was a hero he was unliked because of his potential to free African Americans. Politics and Race Issues caused a catalytic explosion.

Civil War: A Film by Ken Burns, 1990)

But the sparks did not remain at words alone. Congressman Preston Brooks physically fought Senator Charles Sumner on "the floor of the United States Senate." (The Civil War: A Film by Ken Burns, 1990) Although he raised his cane against an abolitionist, the federal government would turn a blind eye. All of these events combined caused more of a clash and desperation to live out their beliefs between the north and the south.

Sometimes conflict is a sign of awakening. The truth of injustice sparks a fire beneath the righteous to fight for liberty.

Southerners were more determined than ever to keep slavery thriving, convincing themselves that it was a good institution, even for the slaves. Northerners were fierier than ever, unwavering in their intention to end slavery once and for all. Both were emotionally and spiritually motivated to uphold their beliefs. There was no way the two could remain one unit before great hostility broke out. Soon after the reestablishment of the slave trade and John Brown's subsequent raid another escalating factor would arise… America received her 16th president.

THE ELECTION OF ABRAHAM LINCOLN

In November 1860, Abraham Lincoln was elected the Republican president by a 40% vote and the already divided nation erupted all the more over this decision. This partition was of course between North and South, but also included varied views in the abolitionist camp. Notable freedom fighters such as Frederick Douglass eventually came to find that the Republican party was not against slavery in new regions of the nation. Instead, they were "opposed to forcing slavery into any Territory of the United States where the white people of that Territory do not want it." (McPherson 9) This insinuates that the party was in fact mainly considering its own interests, not the deeper interests of the problem called slavery.

But some blacks had different views on the Republican party. Unlike Douglass, they believed that "this party was the only major political organization that had taken any kind of a stand

ABRAHAM LINCOLN

Uncommon to popular thought, Abraham Lincoln was not favored by many blacks at the beginning of his election. He appeared adamant that he was for the Union and not necessarily against slavery probably due to fear America would catapult into Civil War.

against slavery, and that a Republican victory would represent a step in the right direction." (McPherson 9-10) If blacks were being represented on any level this was seen as a major victory to these black Republicans. Regardless of whose viewpoint was correct, the Southern states were not pleased with the election of any man who had any form of stance against slavery. This caused a stronger divide between the South and the North.

I would save the Union…If I could save the Union without freeing any slave, I would do it; and if I could save it by freeing all the slaves, I would do it…What I do about Slavery and the colored race, I do because I believe it helps to save this Union."

Abraham Lincoln

Eventually Douglass shared that although Lincoln's election was not the greatest of victories it was a blow at the South. It was outstanding that there was a President in office having any sorts of sentiments towards the black community.

And again, Douglass was right. In February 1861, the South responded to the blow by seceding seven states from the Union, only four months after Lincoln's election,. This was the birthing of the Confederate States of America.

SECESSION FROM THE UNION

Upon Lincoln's election, states begin to secede from the nation. The north and south were divided like never before and the Confederacy was being formulated. In fact, "by the time of his inauguration, 5 months later, just 27 states would remain" in the Union, out of 33 states (The Civil War: A Film by Ken Burns, 1990). The nation appeared to be crumbling bit by bit and people's hearts were restless. Entire military divisions began to leave the Union for the newly established Confederate states. Then it happened. In Montgomery, Alabama, General Jefferson Davis was installed as President over the Confederate States. This inauguration occurred on February 18, 1861.

The new movement was so organic and happened so rapidly that President Jackson's office was described as being housed in "a hotel room a sheet of stationary penned to the door marked the president's office." And when asked about the State Department's meeting location, the secretary of state responded that it was "In my hat, sir, and the archives in my coat pocket." This was a system founded on negro inequality principles. The Vice President quoted, "Our new government is founded upon the great truth that the negro is not equal to the white man." (The Civil War: A Film by Ken Burns, 1990) Of course, such statements reveal the depth of the racial stereotypes of that day. And such intensity would produce more than a moral war.

Two months after President Jackson's election, on April 12th of 1861 at 4:30am, the Civil War commenced. Loud explosions erupted as ammunition fired into the air, sparking the beginnings of America's war between her sundered self. But this fight for the identity of a nation would be well worth it; it was a battle for more than territory or power. It was a clash for humanity, equal rights and liberation. Without this war we would not have the ability to live together in the unity for which we continue to contest.

A WHITE MAN'S WAR

Ironically, in this struggle for freedom, this was not always seen, even by the Union, as the battle's focus. It would take years before blacks were admitted into the military; instead, they were given subservient jobs and considered incompetent for a man's job, like combating. Blacks would face a war within the war. Layers of inequality were present in the midst of this fight for freedom. And, at times, at least for the black community, it appeared that neither the Union nor the Confederacy were completely on her side. She had many smaller battles to fight upon her abolition.

But there were glimpses of hope as great men and women, abolitionists of all sorts, began making strides towards African Americans donning uniform. Although the first sound of fire was ignited by Edmund Ruffin (a "Virginia slave owner") and the north was determined to press against the south, for both the north and south, *this was a white man's war.* (Gates 122) And blacks were not able to exercise their strong desire to combat. They were so desirous to fight for freedom that even Frederick Douglass was on board with fighting through "guerilla bands" and to "descend on the South to destroy slavery." (Gates 122) This was a climatic moment in history. But white leaders such as Lincoln would not allow them to be a part of the Union Army. This must have crushed the African American community at the heart. It was yet another clear example of northern racism.

It is a hard truth, knowing the depth of blatant verbal racism among the leaders of the Union Army. They made it clear they intended for "no niggers" to be in their army and that "this was a white man's war." Even northern politicians like the congressman, Chilton A. White proclaimed, **"This is government of white men, made by white men for white men, to be administered, protected, defended and maintained by white men."** (Gates 123) Although this side of the narrative may not be widely shared, it is important to understand the state of the white community, during that time, not for the sake of shaming, but as unto healing. But even in the midst

GENERAL TUBMAN

Harriet Tubman was more than an abolitionist, she was an Union Army spy. In spite of Congress' resistance, on June 3, 1863 she aided her friend, Col. James Montgomery, in the Combahee River Raid, leading 300 uniformed black men. That day they freed 750 slaves out of slavery!

of crushing rejection, blacks did not give up hope.

One of the wisest voices of the time—black or white—a voice of reason, seemed to be Frederick Douglass who knew that it was inevitable, eventually the Northern Union forces would "be forced to wage war, not just for the Union but against slavery." His and the Weekly Anglo-African's wisdom to wait "for opinions to change" would be prophetic to the direction the North eventually took. Yet some blacks helped the Union army by lesser roles to aid slaves in escaping the "peculiar institution." (Gates 123) In the meantime, many advances were achieved to help black contrabands of war escape slave plantations. All was not loss and truth would eventually win out.

Through a series of interesting events, Congress and a hesitant Lincoln Administration were forced into expediting the process of both protecting and receiving runaway slaves into military complexes. This was due to three slaves who ran away to Fort Monroe in Hampton, Virginia. Upon their escape, Union General Benjamin F. Butler was placed in the awkward position of now receiving many more slaves who found this was a place of safety. When approached by Major John B. Cary due to these three escapees, General Butler brilliantly proclaimed these men contrabands of war. They were considered "fugitives" working for the Union army. This moment was vital in shifting the government to take a stronger stand towards a focus on slavery. "Thus, on August 6, 1861, it passed the first of two Confiscation acts, declaring:

Any property of whatsoever kind or description with intent

to use or employ the same, or suffer the same to be used or
employed, in aiding, abetting, or promoting such
insurrection or resistance to the laws…all such property
is hereby declared to be lawful subject of prize and capture
wherever found; and it shall be the duty of the President of
the United States to cause the same to be seized, confiscated
and condemned." (Gates 124-125)

Fortunately, incredible advances and huge slave escapes wer
achieved such as Robert Smalls journey onto the Planter out o
Charleston. He used his slave training to lead an all-black slave crew
in a covert operation onto Union military territory. They made i
safely out of slavery through sheer intelligence and divine providence
Harriet Tubman also conducted spy work for the Union army in th
Combahee River Raid where she successfully led a two day operation
on June 1 and 2, 1863. In an overnight covert operation she gathered
more than 750 excited slaves onto a ship in South Carolina.

Blacks would unofficially fight in the Civil War before being
legally allowed to do so, because friendly abolitionist Union General
recruited them into battle. For example, in Leavenworth, Kansas
General James H. Lane, went against federal instructions, bringing
in up to 600 black and Indian soldiers on August 4, 1862. This group
of ready soldiers was called the First Kansas Colored Infantry and
fought Confederates in Island Mound Missouri on October 26, 1862
(Gates 130-131).

Unfortunately, the Lincoln Administration and Congress did no
support this type of activity. They shut down efforts of abolitionis

minded generals considering the ex-slaves "fugitives."

Abolitionist General, David Hunter, humorously responded that it would be more correct to consider their former masters the "fugitive rebels." He described black soldiers as "a fine regiment of persons." (Gates 131-132). These were the beginnings of the fight for African American soldiers admittance in the U.S. military.

EMANCIPATING SLAVES AND SOLDIERS

Although many blacks did not trust Lincoln, the Emancipation Proclamation finally did occur in January 1, 1863 and blacks were legally set free from slavery. Gradually history would be reverted in the right direction but not after a lot of bloodshed. Although Lincoln would confess that he was only freeing blacks for the sake of the Union, they were free at last. And celebration would strike the black community. In the words of Frederick Douglass, "We have had a period of darkness…but are now having the dawn of light." (Gates 134)

Still, he could not understand America's deep hypocrisy—at a time when the Union Army was losing the battle against the South and in need of more troops, stating:

"What upon earth is the matter with the American Government and people? Do they really covet the world's ridicule as well as their own social and political ruin? What are they thinking about, or don't they condescend to think at all? So, indeed, it would seem from their blindness in dealing with the tremendous issue now upon them. Was there every anything like it before? They are sorely pressed on every hand by a vast army of slave-holding rebels, flushed with success, and infuriated by the darkest inspirations of a deadly hate, bound to rule or ruin…**Why does the Government reject the negro?"** (McPherson 163-164)

Figure 23 Black Union Army soldiers from the famed 54th Massachusetts Infantry. One of America's first all-black military units.

Upon the Emancipation Proclamation, Lincoln finally allowed black soldiers the opportunity to fight and on January 26, 1863, three weeks after the proclamation, the 54th Massachusetts Infantry became the first all-black infantry in the United States of America. Due to what Henry Louis Gates would describe as their "undeniable performance" 178,000 more black troops were then recruited into the Union army. Due to their involvement, consisting of approximately "10 percent" of the army, the Union military would finally beat the Confederacy, after having reached the point of losing the battle.

REFLECTION QUESTIONS

1. When considering the deaths listed on page 160 and the officers who were not charged for these deaths, how do you think the black community feels? What does this reveal about the mentality of our current legal system towards black deaths? What emotions and concerns may this bring up for black parents?

2. Upon the killing of Alton Sterling, the Bahamian, United Arabs Emirates, and Bahrain governments set out travel advisories to the United States of America. The Bahamas declared that their youth should use "extreme caution" in police interactions. What does this outside perspective reveal to you about the state of our nation today?

3. Have you ever heard of the Philadelphia MOVE bombing? What emotions come to your heart when reading this account? How could events like this have effected black trust towards white police officers? This is something a community tends not to forget.

4. Consider the build-up prior to the Civil War and the justification to resurrect the Slave Trade. Consider the justification to not allow African Americans to fight in the Civil War. What does this reveal about the danger of justifying injustice?

5. Heart Check- Do you tend to categorize blacks as the officer in the MOVE case did? You are not like "them"…Can the words of the black priest help you to let go of preconceived notions about urban, "less civilized" blacks?

6. The question before the Civil War was, "What is stopping any African American from being captured as a slave?" The same question of, "What is stopping any African American from becoming a shooting victim?" is prevalent today. What are your thoughts on how the black community may be feeling about this concept?

7. Pray for true peace that comes from willingness to embrace the hard work of facing our past and confessing our sin. Pray for Jesus' peace in America. Again, we are in a convulsive state.

Chapter 7
Civil Rights

"Every great dream begins with a dreamer. Always remember, you have within you the strength, the patience, and the passion to reach for the stars to change the world."
Harriet Tubman

WE LAUGHED THE PAIN AWAY

We confidently stepped next to a nervous, or at the least discomforted, elderly white woman. But we did not allow her disquieted demeanor to deter us from continuing in lighthearted conversation. "What types of plants are these?" No response. *Well that's strange. Is it because we are different, because I am black?* Let me ask again, maybe I will directly ask her husband. "What types of plants are these?" He finally chooses to respond to me saying, "Oh, this is oregano here… and this is the only kind we cook with all the time…"

Maybe this won't be so bad after all. At least one of them is talking to us. We purchase the oregano and some eggs, asking them to hold them in the cooler at their location so the eggs will not get too warm as we browse the remainder of the items.

After browsing through an antique shop we drove back to the

market where we left our goods. This time I sit in the driver's seat as my sister Lauren retrieves our items. Peeking my head back to the farm couple's booth, I notice she is taking a long time to return to the car. Soon she returns with all our items but the truth pours out. I've definitely heard this type of conversation before...*He said what?*

We laugh the pain away because what was the point of setting them in their place? The whole ordeal was subtle enough to explain away if desired. "He said, 'It's so hot. I used to sit out in the heat all the time and get a sun tan. I would get as *dark as you*. But my wife on the other hand, she would get as red as a lobster. Then she would turn back white."

Lauren chuckles a bit, laughing at this ignorance as his already nervous wife turned red, but not due to the sun this time. "Well, I have been in the sun a lot this summer" she responded. He continues, "Oh, that's not your normal color?" Of course, by this point, Lauren is ready to retreat from this awkward babble and return to the car. I listen wondering how she feels; speechless, feelings of anger rising in my heart.

I know her strength, the fortitude all black women carry, but still my heart ached for the tiny chipping this may have caused in her self-esteem. This one incident weaved perfectly the fluid plight of the black community. Although racism is something we are told to forgive and forget, the trauma is a constant in our daily lives.

That day Lauren's blackness became her strength. In prior years, our blackness became our strength. It became the strength of not only the black community, but America as a whole.

Our blackness became a piece of the American narrative we can be proud of today. All because a few black men and a lot of other folks allowed history's inspiration to break the monstrous sound of fear and discrimination. Instead, they found a way to laugh their pain away. This is the story of the Civil Rights Legacy.

Although racism is something
we are told to forgive and forget,
the trauma is a constant in our daily lives.

PRE-MOVEMENT

Four years can make a serious difference in society, good or bad. In only four years, the Confederate States of America loss their battle to the Union Army as the fight for freedom and liberation emancipated hundreds of slaves from the deep south.

Inclination towards battling injustice also increased in the aftermath of World War II. Hitler's actions towards Jews and his Nazism philosophies set the stage for a stronger awareness of racial injustice. By 1941, A. Philip Randolph led "an all-black movement of 50,000 people" producing the "beginning of mass protests and foreshadowed the tactics of the 1950s and 1960s." (Berry and Blassingame 383)

This was a great move for the black community, a formidable attempt to gain black soldiers equal rights. Of course, this unknowingly set stage for one of the greatest aggregations of black equality, the Civil Rights Movement.

WHITE VS. BLACK VIEWS

Inspite of fiery protest, resistance and clear discomfiture, over half of whites in 1942 chose to believe blacks were content.

The same survey revealed, "six out of ten whites felt Afro-Americans were satisfied, that their status would not improve after the war, and that blacks were completely responsible for their own plight." (Berry and Blassingame 384) Today 38% of whites feel our country has made the changes needed to give blacks equal rights to whites, while only 8% of blacks believe this is true! The mentalities prove to be the same. This thought pattern could not

JUSTICE FIGHTERS

There is new rhetoric that "This is not our grandfather's civil rights movement." And that is due to the pain of not seeing desired change. But Civil Rights leaders modeled a Christian example of boldly speaking up for their community while exemplifying convicting love. This is what we need to be Justice Fighters today.

have been further from the truth; blacks were absolutely resistant to the discrimination and abuse of their human liberties. They were tired of being told to wait and blamed for a situation they as a people group did not ask for nor create.

Our blackness became a piece of the
American narrative we can be proud of today.
All because a few black men and a lot of other folks
allowed history's inspiration to break the monstrous
sound of fear and discrimination. Instead, they
found a way to laugh their pain away.

These two mountains of catalytic thoughts would clash into a volcanic national implosion. Riots began to spring forth in the early to mid-forties over these two ideals that could not seem to be resolved. Tension turned into physical uprisings on the streets of Detroit (1943) and "in 1946 in Tennessee, Alabama, and Pennsylvania." (Berry and Blassingame 384).

Almost a century after the Civil War, a group of ministers rose with King becoming the stunning change agents to a national crisis.

Just as the elderly farmers asking about my sister's "blackness" were blind to their racist bending, white southern moderates failed to see their part in racial wounding. Content to live in their cozy bubble of forward progress, they believed blacks were extreme to ask for sudden change. This was too hasty. *Why didn't blacks understand? Laws had to be changed, people's hearts to be bended and it just wasn't that simple?* Patience was surely in order.

But one factor was not considered, the conditions, the daily emotional and psychological trauma blacks faced, **not to mention the generational marks left on every element of the black community.** They had sat, waiting for change, making small advancements while enduring inevitable set-backs for almost a century. Perhaps, just as in slavery times, blacks had a greater awareness of the actual moral state of the nation. Due to their heightened self-awareness, blacks were able to see into their oppressor's heart. This

MODERATE VIEWS

Moderate whites were apathetic. They ignored the problem of their day rather than addressing it. Today we fight militants because of international tragedies but being a moderate isn't a solution either. Asking blacks to be "patient" while not providing solutions is not the answer. To not take a stand against wrong is siding with injustice.

caused them to accurately gauge the severity of resistance that would be needed for the formidable giant, Racism, to come tumbling down.

In 1942 "six out of ten whites felt Afro-Americans were satisfied, that their status would not improve after the war, and that blacks were completely responsible for their own plight."

FROZEN VIEWS

In 1942, 6 out of 10 whites felt blacks were responsible for their current state. Sometimes we assume that it is okay to blame African Americans of not forgiving or being bitter, maybe even trying to rekindle strife. But the same rhetoric was given in 1942, at a time when we can look back saying, "Blacks were definitely not treated fairly." This perspective has been streamlined over centuries, regardless of current events, or long after slavery's annulment. The reality is blacks have been blamed while dismissing the past's effects for many years.

A SPIRITUAL HERITAGE

Over the years, blacks have invested in this great democracy more than any other group excluding the Native Americans. A determined people, a people of faith and wonderful resilience, their forgiveness was transcendent of the world we know. America's progress was carried upon the shoulders of her dark- skinned slave and Civil War heroes.

Blacks have invested in this great democracy more than any other group excluding Native Americans. A determined people, a people of faith and wonderful resilience, their forgiveness was transcendent of the world we know.

Choosing the way of love, an entire people group would become a testament of the Messianic theme, *pointing all of humanity to a higher ethical standard.* Their righteousness would spring forth like the dawn, exposing a heart of unconditional charity. In the theme of Maya Angelou's, *Still I Rise*, black men, women, boys and girls would rise to the dignity of the occasion, becoming a choir of saintly figurines.

The principles upon which they stood were generational blessings, passed down from slaves **who learned to give when nothing in this natural world gave reason to continue.** Slaves stayed up all day, and pressed all night into an abundance of light—the sort that thrived in slave spirituals driving us on to freedom.

One such heir of this blessing was the honorable Ambassador Andrew Young. His family was, perhaps, a microcosm of common mentalities groomed in the black community throughout centuries of cruel oppression. Soon, men like Young, proved to a worldwide audience what it meant to "turn the other cheek" and "love thy enemies."

THE WHY BEHIND THE MOVEMENT: JIM CROW

Many times Jim Crow is looked at from a discourteous angle, many times by the white community, minimizing at least, denouncing at most, the depth of psychological anguish the black community continues to relive. Mirroring the colonization of Africa, this evil giant spread throughout the south within a "thirty to fifty-year" timespan shocking relations between blacks and whites afresh. (Berry and Blassingame 349). Although progress had been made, it was another crafty evolution of slavery in America.

JIM CROW ETIQUETTE

One author eloquently defines these systematic relations as "Jim Crow Etiquette Norms." These norms came justified by the white church, teaching professionals, scholars, media and government officials. Both the school systems and activities of white youth reflected "anti-black stereotypes."[13] This "new" order continued a systematically racist mentality, a doctrine, that because blacks were inclined toward negative, even dangerous behaviors, they must be treated with greater force, stricter laws, more caution and at times inhumane violence.

The norms created in this system are enough to aid us in imagining the emotions and thoughts any human treated likewise would feel.

Due to the common assent that "whites were superior to blacks in all important ways, a collection of standards was developed to control the mentalities and actions of the black community:

"a. A black male could not offer his hand (to shake hands) with a white male because it implied being socially equal. Obviously, a black male could not offer his hand or any other part of his body to a white woman, because

POSITIONING PERSPECTIVE

Blacks have a precious view of their condition, they see it from the inside out. And they have a great vantage point of the white community that is oftentimes dismissed. It takes humility to listen when you do not have to, but in slavery times and possibly now they were right about the moral state of our nation.

he risked being accused of rape.

b. Blacks and whites were not supposed to eat together. If they did eat together, whites were to be served first, and some sort of partition was to be placed between them.

c. Under no circumstance was a black male to offer to light the cigarette of a white female—that gesture implied intimacy.

d. Blacks were not allowed to show public affection toward one another in public, especially kissing, because it offended whites.

e. Jim Crow etiquette prescribed that blacks were introduced to whites, never whites to blacks. For example, "Mr. Peters (the white person), this is Charlie (the black person), that I spoke to you about."

f. Whites did not use courtesy titles of respect when referring to blacks, for example, Mr., Mrs., Miss., Sir, or Ma'am. Instead, blacks were called by their first names. Blacks had to use courtesy titles when referring to whites, and were not allowed to call them by their first names.

g. If a black person rode in a car driven by a white person, the black person sat in the back seat, or the back of a truck.

h. White motorists had the right-of-way at all intersections." (Jim Crow Museum article)

JIM CROW'S EFFECTS ON BLACK MEN

As aforementioned, manhood was infamously stolen when husbands were torn from their wives and children or could not protect their beloved brides from the sexual assault of white men. This was compounded by withdrawing rights to "show public affection" towards her or look into the eyes of a white man.

Their adulthood was also depressed by whites refusing to show a basic level of respect by referring to the most honor-worthy blacks with the basic title of Mr. or Mrs, Sir or Ma'am. What would this do to the children watching as another era of black parents were treated inhumanely due to the color of their skin?

As a black woman, I'm only one black woman, but I've noticed it is hard to find public affection in the black church, home and public square. We have learned to be strong, we have had to be strong but being affectionate and gentle was a stolen quality. Now we are relearning how to give and receive this type of love.

HAVE BLACKS FORGIVEN?

Forgiveness and the Black community is inexorably tied together. Remembering slave stories full of letting go of a lifetime of abuse, civil rights leaders turning the other cheek and parents choosing not to retaliate as their children silently suffered is crucial to finding modern unity. Before quickly accusing blacks of not forgiving, grace is needed. How much has she endured? What is her history? Acknowledging this rich legacy is important if we want to inspire her to keep on in the fight of Forgiveness now.

SEPARATE BUT EQUAL?

Out of determination to dishonor black rights, another legal loophole was created. The 1896 Plessy v. Ferguson legalization threatened the hope of being "free." Unfortunately, this law "legitimized Jim Crow laws and the Jim Crow way of life." (Jim Crow Museum article).

As more laws such as Louisiana's "Separate Car Law" (1890) were enforced, Southern minds began to gradually rehearse the idea of "separate but equal." Blacks were also strategically banned from equal opportunities, like voting, through impossible "grandfather clauses" and "literacy tests".

The paradox to this demand for "separate but equal" is how much blacks and whites were inseparable in their daily lives. Blacks served whites as "maids and menials in white homes, public accommodations, and other businesses." (Oates 58) An evolution of the slave system was institutionalized in the south. Whites did not want blacks in their world in *an evenly matched custom-* through formal legalities, unspoken codes of conduct and physical force, both militant and moderate whites would do everything within their power to *keep blacks in their place.*

Blacks are still kept in their place today. I have a friend whose mother was a maid in New Jersey for many years. She worked all those years for rich white families in the most racist areas. I remember feeling so bad that she experienced that type of a life, "What would it have been like to be considered subservient?" It was hard not to think back to slavery times.

Then there were the maids of my adulthood. Taking walks through Buckhead, an affluent area of Atlanta, Georgia, I would watch these young black girls come out of beautiful homes, nannying white families' children.

And then there was the job I took as a preschool teacher. For a moment in time, I got a glimpse of what it must have been like for Civil Rights women. There were older women watching doctors, psychologists, and upper middle class white children all day long. My heart panged to see them find another role in society. It was hard not to think about the past. The moral of the story: we still remember our history and it effects our current times. This was our place and, by many, we are expected to stay in those spaces.

JIM CROW'S EFFECTS ON CHILDREN

Finally, the Supreme Court confirmed the trauma of these "separate but equal"

RESPECT AS A NEED

Just as we have a need for air, water, food and shelter, we have relational needs. One of them is Respect. When we intentionally remove respect from a people group for centuries, this respect must be intentionally re-given. Respect is simply valuing and esteeming highly another person. This starts with our heart and then with our actions.

facilities across the South in its May 17, 1954 case stating:

"Segregation of white and colored children in public schools has a detrimental effect upon the colored children...*A sense of inferiority affects the motivation of a child to learn. Segregation with the sanction of law, therefore, has a tendency to [retard] the educational and mental development of Negro children*...We conclude that, in the field of public education, the doctrine of "separate but equal" has no place. Separate educational facilities are inherently unequal."[14]

VIOLENCE AND LYNCHING'S OF BLACKS

Although a legislative victory had been won, violence became one of the greatest threats to the black community. Oftentimes this factor deterred blacks from fighting for their rights legally in court or physically through public

SENSORING INFERIORITY

Psychology proves that children struggle due to "a sense of inferiority." I remember my brother's guidance counselor telling him he could not go to a four-year college and needed to look into a local college instead. But he went on to become an engineer accepted into Drexel University. Other black young men feel hindered by the world's perspective as well. Inferiority is real.

---

14 Brown v. Board of Education article, www.civilrights.org /education/brown/ brown.html)

boycotting. The violence and lynching of blacks became the harness whites either promoted or allowed to keep blacks tame. There are reports of as many as "4,730 known lynchings, including 3,440 black men and women" between the years 1882 and 1986. [15]

Moderates in the white south, who claimed dis-involvement in such behavior, did not choose to stop it, convincing themselves that blacks needed more patience to change their current world. Moderatism was not their only cancer; fear was also entrenched in the hearts of whites, believing blacks were dangerous and sexually heightened. The result was unwarranted mob violence or what Gunnar Myrdal (1944) would deem "a terrorization or massacre…a mass lynching."[16]

AWAKENING A SLEEPING GIANT

We have all probably seen the bully scene. The proverbial school-boy giant, taunts his smaller classmate for his style, his personality, and anything else he can devise; the heckled boy returns home lamenting to his parents. Comforted and taught to defend himself, he walks into the school, head held high he advances straight towards Goliath's big, strong body ready to let him have it. Goliath, in shock at his humble enemy's newfound boldness, declares chilling jokes, even pushing his normally subservient victim to the side. Davy's petite body tumbles to the floor in dismay as he hears his mother's cry, "Don't let Goliath keep pushing you around. Look him straight

---

[15] www.ferris.edu/jimcrow/what.htm
[16] (Myrdal 556, *An American dilemma: the Negro problem and modern democracy*)

in the eye, like this!" He can still see his mother standing square in front of him with a face so fierce the greatest of armies would fall back in retreat. "Put him in his place once and for all. You'll see. He'll back off!"

Today is the day. He decides to take heed to his caring mother's advice. He will no longer be pushed around. No more turn overs. Turned over food trays, desks, homework papers. Soon his humble, direct resistance would keep Goliath's attacks at bay. And his view of his self would heighten as he chose to stand his ground.

AMERICA'S CATALYST, ROSA PARKS

This Davy-effect occurred the day Rosa Parks decided that enough was enough. No longer would she sit in submissive silence; because, there is a point when your submission becomes abuse. Although debatable whether she was "planted there by the NAACP" as some authors claim, Mrs. Parks movement would become a classic day

FACING FEAR

Walking into a crowd of "the other" can be scary. All women. All men. All Hispanics. All Asians. All Blacks. All white. And then you. But it's so important to remember that once we bridge the gaps by facing fears we normalize the faulty thinking saying "Don't go talk to her. She's not like you." And the bonding begins.

in American history.

Alike little Davy, Mrs. Parks decided to push her bully back, but not by physical force. She used the art of declination. On December 1, 1955, her Montgomery bus was in for a surprise as she quietly pledged to stay where she belonged—at the front of the bus. Mrs. Parks *would not be moved.*

Why should she when she deserved to sit in the front alike all American citizens? Her brave move in the face of being jailed at least, lynched at worse, was what it took to catalyze an unexpected trail of coming events.

This sole act created immense tension, but it was the beginning of the awakening. The awakening of an already agitated giant. That day white privilege was being challenged, causing even moderate whites to feel discomforted. It was humbling to be in a situation where a black woman even assumed a position of equality.

SIT LIKE ROSA DID

Rosa Parks decided to push her bully back, but not by physical force. She chose not to be moved. Today we can make the same unpopular decision to sit in seats of authority until we are physically removed. Sometimes when light comes into darkness the darkness becomes exposed. People begin to see their hearts and it can be Really Uncomfortable. But as you sit, sit still, in faith. Things will begin to change. People will begin in integrate. And truth will be exposed.

But God used this black woman. He took her out of obscurity, brought her to a place of notoriety then used it to stir the black community out of her "apathy." (Carson 51) This would be made possible through the work of E.D. Nixon. Nixon was a resilient African American leader and the "state president of the NAACP," one of the radiant rays in a cosmos of gloomy disarray (Carson 51). He contacted Dr. King on December 2nd sharing Mrs. Parks narrative to which Dr. King was stunned. Nixon then added a contemplation that would change history, "I feel that the time has come to boycott the buses. Only through a boycott can we make it clear to the white folks that we will not accept this type of treatment any longer." (Carson 51)

Dr. King had received his charge and was suddenly swept into the organization of a city-wide bus boycott. In response, he talked with a fellow pastor, Ralph David Abernathy and together they orchestrated an assembly

WE WON'T JUST SIT HERE

We can sit like Rosa but at some point we do have to get up, speak up and do something else. E.D. Nixon said "Only through a boycott can we make it clear to the white folks that we will not accept this type of treatment any longer." Being non-violent is essential, but taking a stand is just as vital.

of Christian and city leaders into King's church. There, they develop the boycott terms and publicized their "mass meeting…at Holt Street Baptist Church." (Carson 52) Evidently this boycott was in God's providence because "every Negro taxi company in Montgomery had agreed to support the protest." (Carson 54)

God can take our hidden stories
and use them to shake nations when
He desires to place them in the ears of kings.

In response to Mrs. Park's arrest, the Montgomery Improvement Association (MIA) was also formed. Dr. King was elected as the president of the MIA by an uncontested vote. His acceptance of this role was furthermore an act of God because he had turned down an opportunity to lead his community NAACP so he could focus on school and his new church responsibilities. Due to this decision, he was available at this critical historical moment to take leadership of this new movement as the MIA leader.

And lead he did, but not with force or arrogance; instead, he chose a more noble form of leadership. He led the people constantly reminding the world that the real heroes were the men, women and children who were willing to sacrifice without notoriety or fame.

A RISING KING

It was time for change. Through an unusual turn of events, King became the pilot to this turbulent fight right on cue. He embodied the only missing element, *clearly defined leadership.*

For years, a strong fear (not without reason) clasped and tried to crush the black south. Yet, the people continued to stand under civil oppression. One must realize that upon the long-awaited consummation of the Civil War and the Emancipation Proclamation, living in the south was still not idealistic if you were "colored." Even well known, respected men like Booker T. Washington's lives were on the line. There are accounts of men so afraid of the "Ku Klux Klan" that they chose to dwell in their "attic surrounded by…guns." (Berry and Blassingame 372) Blacks were also described as living "in a state of dread and suspense." (Berry and Blassingame 372)

Even today, blacks have to deal with real fears. Just recently I was on a business trip with my husband in Chattanooga, TN. I dropped him off then went off for some "me time" at a local Target. The GPS was so wonderful that I ended up in the back gravel roads of Tennessee mountains searching for a Target store.

It was scary, to say the least. Images of the Ku Klux Klan and Confederate flags (appearing more and more in our southern neighborhoods) began to flash before me. I had to think positive, keep my eyes on the road and get out as quick as possible. It's sad that we experience these types of day-to-day flashbacks. But it is more common than many would imagine.

King was called to bring peace to the fears of people in his day. But before King gave a sense of calm resolve to the black community, as the face of an international movement, he was a pastor of a sweet congregation-Dexter Baptists in Montgomery, Alabama. He was trained by his upbringing and content to use that in conjunction with educational instruction to learn the art of pastoring.

Additionally, he a genius in organizational development and community reformation. Joining with NAACP efforts, King led campaigns for "social-action" "to tend the sick and needy, help artists with promise, and administer scholarship funds for high-school graduates," all out of his local church. (Oates 57) These early years became the groundwork for a grander plan to come.

Soon King became a key leader on the NAACP city organization and he joined the Alabama Council on Human Relations, "the only interracial group in town," a move reflective of his heart to converge

TODAY'S NEED: CLEARLY DEFINED LEADERSHIP

Today we have a lot of voices and cries for help, just as was heard by the children of Israel when in bondage to Egypt. But we are in need of Moses'. Some say there will be many Moses' others believe there is a Moses God will raise up to heal our crisis. Either way, we could use a dose of clear, patient, educated, prepared and loving leaders to speak into our current issues. *Could you be called to make this difference within your realm of influence?*

blacks and whites. (Oates 58) He grieved the lack of unity between church leaders of varying nationalities.

Unfortunately, there was an understandable reason for this divisiveness. It was the same basis for the segregation prevailing throughout southern states, Caucasians simply avoided having association alongside African American pastors in an egalitarian approach. Instead, the code of Jim Crow ethics, ensured the white community find a way to afflict blacks with a lesser placement in society.

There are accounts of men so afraid of the "Ku Klux Klan" that they chose to dwell in their "attic surrounded by guns."

DISCONTENTMENT AND FRICTION

Unfortunately, not all were ready. Blacks were described as "complacent and terribly afraid of angering the white man." King described some as having a "corroding sense of inferiority, which often expressed itself in a lack self-respect." (Oates 58) Even black ministers were trapped in this web of unholy acceptance. Great need for a catalyst existed rising above the constant chipping away of black morale. Their spirits needed to be both healed and challenged. But underneath this passivity was a brewing resolve to challenge the current system.

The year was 1955. By this point, the black community had enough of the names, "monkeys," "apes," "niggers," "black cows" and being disregarded, bending under the real threats of lynchings or unwarranted incarceration. Along with name calling, "the drivers particularly singled out black women for abuse." (Oates 63) The legal, physical and emotional wear was coming to head. No form of restitution or accountability for white men's misconduct, was being had…all the while white moderates and militants told blacks to wait for change.

But spiritual leaders such as Dr. King were able to help infuse a revived religious fervor in the temperament of a previously subdued people. Operating in the spirit forefathers of the Underground Railroad did, they rose out of subservient slumber. *In A Stone of Hope*, author David Chappell, describes this new phenomenon:

> "…a whole new generation suddenly got the idea into its collective head that wildly idealistic visions of social justice were realistic—and worth the trouble to pursue. Can this be equated with the Second Great Awakening of the mid-nineteenth century, which spurred abolitionism and other radical reform movements?" (Chappell 101)

Historical lessons *would awaken the black community*, as organic church-schools formed, to teach the next generation, filling students with fresh hope as they marched into a new form of war. Nonviolent Resistance. But non-violent did not mean non-responsive. These warriors chose to act upon deep belief, knowing that faith without works is dead. For the understanding of our past has always been a determining factor in the undeniable courage of the black community, motivating us to progress out of passivity into the current era's need for change. And that is what occurred throughout the Civil Rights Movement.

THE BIRMINGHAM CAMPAIGN

In January 1963, a few years after the Montgomery Awakening (A Civil Rights movement in Montgomery, Alabama), "King publicly announced that he was going to Birmingham and that he would lead demonstrations there until "Pharaoh let God's people go." (Oates 213) This time a fiery minister named, Fred Shuttlesworth, called Dr. King to his city. Shuttlesworth's Alabama Christian Movement for Human Rights (ACMHR) and King's SCLC joined to fight the strongest battle yet against one of the strongest segregationist police commissioners in the south, Bull Connor. Conner vowed that "blood would run in the streets" before Birmingham would desegregate." (Oates 212)

King and his preacher friends would create a "model" to tear down their day's racial disparities, including Bull Connor's tactics. One of these leaders was Ambassador Andrew Young, who described the next move to Birmingham, AL as the "turning point" of the movement and Dr. King's full acceptance of his mantle as leader of the Civil Rights Movement.

Non-violent did not mean Non-responsive. They chose to act on what they believed, knowing that faith without works is dead.

While their previous campaigns across the south were somewhat "sporadic," Young stated that "Birmingham was a movement that Martin Luther King anticipated, planned, and coordinated from beginning to end."(Young 186)

By the beginning of the year (January 1963) Dr. King declared an equally adamant response to Connor; he intended to campaign until "Pharaoh let's God's people go." (Oates 213)

But again, he found a sleeping black community and had to do the hard work of rustling them to performance. He continued to challenge a prejudice police force, commanding them to action with his weapon of choice, peaceful resistance. King's "Birmingham Manifesto" clearly detailed the black community's expectations:

"all lunch counters, restrooms and drinking fountains in downtown department and variety stores be desegregated, that Negroes be hired in local businesses and industry, and that a biracial committee be established to work out a schedule for desegregation in other areas of city life." (Oates 216)

Dr. King did not have lighthearted expectations for the City of Birmingham. He was very specific in his "demands." In the face of an ornery, determined and segregationist police commissioner, Bull Conner, King was neither intimidated nor backing down. His unperturbed example further inspired Birmingham's previously quieted blacks to action.

Eventually small groups of "ten and twenty" blacks around his vision, went to his nonviolent interactive training classes and occupied the front lines. This group then grew to 65 willing activists. This is how he spurred the movement ahead in spite of great white, and sometimes black, resistance.

LEGAL CHANGES

Civil Rights leaders relied on the NAACP to help direct needed legal changes. Today there are laws that can help the black community progress. We change legislation through clear demands, not through ambiguity. Knowing our needs in foster care, adoption and education, is the beginning of fostering change.

LET MY PEOPLE GO

The words, "Let my people go" became a thematic rhythm to every Civil Rights Campaign. The same elements as the Jewish Exodus were at play: a minister of God, formerly complacent people, an abusive Pharaoh-system, Divine strategy and the Sovereign hand of God. Impossibility became tangible as all these factors combined in shaking America to its core. This is the politically correct game many in white establishments have played for many years, but at its core it is simply, racism.

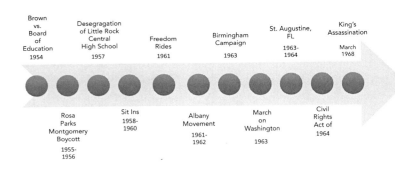

Figure 24 Timeline of the Civil Rights Movement, 1954-1968

But King's Exodus added the plague of direct action through the means of sit ins, stand ins, mass marches, boycotts, freedom rides and integration. Like Pharaoh's tactics, many times whites flat out lied to blacks telling them they were going to receive their deliverance if they would just be patient. But deep in their hearts, they knew an impossible legal process was in place to hinder these promises from ever occurring.

DIRECT ACTION

Groups like Freedom Riders also used direct action to resist these laws. For example, in response to the Boynton v. Virginia decision of 1960, outlawing segregation in highway traveling, Freedom Riders rode through southern roads purposefully, determined to activate the court approved removal of segregated restrooms, water fountains, buses, counters and trains. That spring Freedom Riders gained international attention. These pioneer riders paid the costly price of being beat mercilessly by white segregationists. In response, the Kennedy Administration implemented an "Interstate Commerce Commission (ICC) order…expressly prohibiting segregated facilities in interstate travel." (Young 164-165)

BREAK THE INJUNCTION

Although only 65 people responded to King's initial call, Civil Rights history was made when he demanded the desegregation of economic localities such as stores, restrooms, and water fountains in

HISTORICAL STRATEGY: ORGANIC TOOLS

Because of the educational crisis on race in our nation, we need Organic Schools. These school were historically housed in black churches, but this type of teaching has fallen away over the years. In an attempt not to over-focus on race issues we have an entire generation uneducated in how we arrived where we are today. Teaching our past prepares us, give us wisdom, courage and hope for current problems. We deserve to know how we overcame and can continue to overcome today.

his "Birmingham Manifesto." (Oates 216). News interests began to peak as they conducted their campaign.

Finally, King chose to "break the injunction," placed on him- sentencing him to jail if he continued protesting. Unfortunately, after publicly declaring he would break this injunction, he found his financers had no more bail money. King was in a dilemma. Consulting with his leaders and praying, he decided to enter the jail sentence saying, "I'm going to jail...I don't know what will happen. I don't know where the money will come from. But I have to make a faith act."

The next day he was jailed in Birmingham for breaking this order. It was during solitary confinement that he wrote one of his most famous pieces to white reverends, his "Letter from Birmingham Jail." And while he was in jail, A.D. (his brother) conducted a march of 1500 blacks. (Oates 219-221)

NON-VIOLENT RESISTANCE

In the civil-rights movement non-violent tactics were used to make a statement. The sam can work today through:
Sit Ins
Strikes
Letters
Vigils
Petitions
Walks
Marches
Rallies
Boycotts &
Civil Disobedience

It is possible to mal a difference withou violence.

OUT OF THE MOUTH OF BABES: "WE WANT FEE-DOM!"

The movement continued even throughout King's imprisonment but not without its challenges to stay alive. Upon his release, the movement was barely breathing; in fact, it was falling to pieces. With this setback King had a choice- succumb to bitter failure or find another open door. He was told that high school students were becoming active in the movement. Should children be brought into such a dangerous battle? After discussing with his leader's they decided that not only should the children enter the war, but this was the perfect strategy to break Birmingham's stubborn back. This was another drastic step of faith as children made history, marching the streets for "Fee-dom!"

These fired-up children saw it as an honor to go to jail. Images of them fearlessly marching into jails stormed the press. They were excited to be locked up for what one child would declare was, "Fee-dom!" It started with about 1,000 children walking into Sixteenth

COMMITTING TO THE CAUSE & THE COST

If we want to see lasting generational change it's going to take strong commitment to the cause. We have to be willing to sacrifice how we look to others for the sake of seeing hope restored and relationships reconciled. Although we have had the support of family, it has not been easy to explain why we chose to integrate white circles. But we knew that is what it was going to take to make a difference. Likewise, you may be called to integrate black circles to be a part of the solution.

Ferguson Dilemma

Street Baptist Church. True to character, Bull Connor thoughtlessly treated them as adults.

With an international audience watching, he packed them into Birmingham's jail cells.

Connor even used forceful fire-hoses to put these children back into their place. The children were left "crying and bloodied" in the street as german shepherds were used to intimidate them all away. (Oates 232-235)

By May 5th, this peaceful army of children had rose from 1,000 to 2,500 to now 3,000 youth conducting a prayer walk straight to Birmingham jail. As Connor told his officers to strike them again with fire-hoses the officers refused and are accounted to have fell back weeping. (Oates 236-237) Finally real results were occurring. Consequently, powerful men such as "Robert Kennedy's Assistant Attorney General for Civil Rights" arrived in Birmingham to establish an agreement. (Oates 235)

THE BIRMINGHAM MANIFESTO: CHANGE YOU CAN'T IGNORE

City leaders agreed that they needed to come to peace as a group, outside of Connor's leadership. For 72 hours, they met devising a plan that would be agreeable to the black community. On Friday, May 10, an agreement, for all aspects of the Manifesto, was made in Birmingham. And by the 23rd of May, the Alabama Supreme Court removed Connor from office.

This victory was so successful that there was no more room for

Pharaoh's shaky promises. It is reported that

> "the library, municipal golf courses, public buildings, and finally even the schools themselves...local merchants at last removed "WHITE" and "COLORED" signs on drinking fountains and restrooms, opened downtown lunch counters to Birmingham's long-suffering Negroes, and even hired some in hitherto whites-only positions." (Oates 242)

WE'RE ON TO CANAAN LAND!

The lack of administration in former movements like Albany's campaigns and inevitable criticism of the SCLC had been redeemed. There was no doubt about it; King had been sent to America for such a time as this. The Red Sea was open, our people marched through and were continuing to Canaan Land.

There are other victories King led his people to fulfill, time would fail us to tell of them all in this short summarization of a lengthy tale. But the values behind this movement remained the same in each location: the fight for Justice, Loving one's enemies, Forgiveness, Nonviolence, Self-Dignity and High Expectations. By the end of the movement, it was clear that the black community had been, once again, a great example of integrity, forgiveness and following Biblical commandments **to win their rightful place as brothers and sisters in a once foreign land.**

REFLECTION QUESTIONS

1. Have you ever been in a situation where you realized a comment you made was racist? What did you learn from this experience?
2. Have you ever been in a situation where you were racially mistreated? How did this make you feel and how did you handle it?
3. There was a lack of strength to speak up and rightfully so, in the face of mass lynching. It took strong leadership to awaken America to her need for change. Where do we need clearly defined leadership to today's racial climate?
4. The black community's rich history was a springboard to many activists being martyred for the sake of equality. How do you think knowing America's racial history could help today's people to shift perspectives?
5. During King's Birmingham jail sentence, the movement seemed to come to a screeching halt. What can we learn about King's resilient fight for freedom?

Conclusion

The last few years have been a crazy mix of unexpected life transitions, national events and deeper insights. We never planned to move from the urban core of Atlanta to a predominantly white Southern Baptist church in Marietta, GA. Tensions have historically been high between blacks and the Southern Baptist but perhaps this could be an answer to Dr. Martin Luther King's cry to the white church in Birmingham Jail. Our nation has also seemed to roll into a tumultuous racial and political divide reminiscent of days prior to the Civil War. Social media erupted with so many questions, angry rants, heated debates over domino riots filling our tv screens. In the midst of this crisis, a group of young 20-something historically black college students move into a conservative white environment. This would be interesting.

Social media erupted with so many questions, angry rants, heated debates over domino riots filling our screens. The elephant in the room was being exposed forcing the next generation of black youth not only into America's shaky streets but into a journey of self-discovery.

Conclusion

They learned about pre-slavery Africa, the Middle Passage, America's past with 400 years of chattel slavery, the Abolitionist Movement, Civil War heroes, and the Civil Rights Movement. Both black and white youth began to wrestle with this past. Maybe it doesn't matter. Maybe it should remain buried. Maybe we never made the progress we thought. Maybe the answer is militancy. Maybe race is just a distraction.

All these ideas continue to volley back and forth and *The Ferguson Dilemma* is a small attempt to join this national discussion. Because we know that all it will take is one spark to light a fire again.

Perhaps we can mourn our past, celebrate our progress, admit our wrong and look forward to a bright future. If we have the hard talks and look through the lens of unconditional love I believe with all my heart we are on the wings of healing.

So, to all my American friends, brothers and sisters, black, white and in between please don't give up the hope of being one. Too much has been sacrificed, too much blood shed, too many people jailed, too many prayers prayed and spirituals sung for us to give up the dream prematurely. It is time for the next generation of national leaders to emerge and take the reins of educated influence. *Could you be the answer to The Ferguson Dilemma?*

Sources

Chapter 2: Colonization Affects Us Now

1. A. Adu Boahen. *African Perspectives of Colonialism.* Johns Hopkins University Press, 1989.
2. John Reader. *Africa: A Biography of the Continent.* Knopf Publishing Group, 1998.
3. Horton, James Oliver and Lois E. Horton. *Hard Road to Freedom: The Story of African America, Volume I: African Roots through the Civil War.* Rutgers University Press, 2002.
4. Anne Phillips. T*he Enigma of Colonialism: British Policy in West Africa.* Indiana University Press, 1989.
5. Berry, Mary Frances and John W. Blassingame. *Long Memory The Black Experience in America.* Oxford University Press, 1982.

Chapter 3: Middle Passages

1. John Reader. *Africa: A Biography of the Continent.* Knopf Publishing Group, 1998.
2. Joy DeGruy. *Post Traumatic Slave Syndrome: America's Legacy of Enduring Injury and Healing.* Uptone Press, 2005.
3. Franklin, John Hope and Alfred A. Moss, Jr. *From Slavery to Freedom: A History of African Americans.* McGraw-Hill, 1988.
4. Horton, James Oliver and Lois E. Horton. *Hard Road to Freedom: The Story of African America, Volume I: African Roots through the Civil War.* Rutgers University Press, 2002.
5. Ouladah Equiano. *Great Journeys Sold as a Slave.* Penguin UK, 2007

6. Williams John A. and Charles F. Harris. *Amistad 1: Writings on Black History and Culture.* Random House, 1970.
7. Truth, Sojourner and Painter, Nell Irvin. *Narrative of Sojourner Truth.* Penguin Classics, 1998.

Chapter 5: Emancipate Us

1. David Brion Davis. *The Problem of Slavery in the Age of Emancipation.* Vintage, 2015.
2. Barbour Publishing. *Inspiring Women of the Faith.* Barbour Books, 2009.
3. Berry, Mary Frances and John W. Blassingame. *Long Memory: The Black Experience in America.* Oxford University Press, 1982.

Chapter 6: Civil Wars

1. David Brion Davis. *The Problem of Slavery in the Age of Emancipation.* Vintage, 2015.
2. *The Civil War: A Film by Ken Burns.* Directed by Ken Burns,1990
3. Henry Louis Gates. *Life Upon These Shores: Looking at African American History, 1513-2008.* Knopf, 2013.
4. David S. Reynolds. John Brown, Abolitionist: The Man Who Killed Slavery, Sparked the Civil War, and Seeded Civil Rights. Vintage, 2006.
5. James M. McPherson. *Tried by War: Abraham Lincoln as Commander in Chief.* Penguin Books, 2009.

6. James M. McPherson. *The Negro's Civil War: How American Blacks Felt and Acted During the War for the Union.* Vintage Books, 2003.

Chapter 7: Civil Rights

1. Berry, Mary Frances and John W. Blassingame. *Long Memory: The Black Experience in America.* Oxford University Press, 1982.

2. Pilgrim, David. "Jim Crow Museum: Origins of Jim Crow." *Jim Crow Museum of Racist Memorabilia,* Ferris State University, Sept. 2000, ferris.edu/news/jimcrow/what.htm. Accessed 8 August 2016.

3. Stephen B. Oates. *Let the Trumpet Sound: A Life of Martin Luther King, Jr.* Harper Perennial, 2013.

4. Myrdal, Gunnar. *An American Dilemma: The Negro Problem and Modern Democracy.* Transaction Publishers, 1995. Clayborne Carson. *The Autobiography of Martin Luther King Jr.* Warner Books, 2001.

5. David L. Chappell. *A Stone of Hope: Prophetic Religion and the Death of Jim Crow.* The University of North Carolina Press, 2005.

6. Andrew Young. *An Easy Burden: The Civil Rights Movement and the Transformation of America.* Baylor University Press, 2008.

Additional Resources

CONVERGENCE MOVEMENT

Convergence is a prayer and mission's movement launching Generational Influencers from Campuses to Inner Cities to the ends of the Earth. This gathering of next gen influencers share the skills of multicultural and generational engagement with the body of Christ. These leaders are committed to modeling and establishing healthy relationships in a day where 1 out of 3 children live without a father, more than 1/3rd of millennials are unaffiliated with any faith, and 72% of blacks are fatherless. 43% of blacks and 11% of whites believe our country will not make changes needed for equality. Embracing Diversity and Honing Generational Skills is the answer. See ConvergenceMovement.com for more info.

Learn to heal racial divides, rebuild the African American community, and interact cross culturally in a diverse environment. Our emphasis on healing the black community through education, collaboration, and converging resources will prepare your church or leaders to gain practical momentum towards non-offensive impact.

CSM Webinars: Online training on cross cultural and generational engagement.
Convergence Talks: Bring a CSM speaker to your church, small group or organization.
Student Enrollment: Join CSM for a 3 month, 12 month or 3-year tract.

Launching September 2017. See **ConvergenceMovement.com** for more information.

SUMMER INTERNSHIP

The Convergence Summer Internship is a two-month tract inviting various cultures, denominations and generations to merge in leadership development learning to

Engage Cross Culturally

Understand Racial Issues

Build Relational Skillsets, &

Emerge in their Sphere of Influence.

This hands-on experience will prepare you to lead more sensitively in your current circle of impact while carrying new experiences that help build bridges in needed areas.

Please see **ConvergenceMovement.com** for dates, location and registration.

WIFE • EDUCATOR • WRITER • SPEAKER • PASTOR • SOCIAL ENTREPRENEUR

JadeLee.org is a 501c3 organization with the purposes of providing resources for the church, black diaspora and women in an age of cultural divisiveness and needed skillsets to cross racial barriers. These educational aids help leaders with the competency needed to Biblically engage untapped cultures.

JLO also hosts community boosting events that stimulate economic growth, job opportunities and education in the black community such as Career Fairs, Business Expos, Beauty Fairs, and an annual Women's Leadership Academy.

Find more books and free eBooks at **JadeLee.org**

About the Author

Jade Lee is a writer and pastor's wife from Atlanta, GA. She has been writing on race issues and healing for the past 10 years. Her husband, Corey, and her are both Hampton University graduates, Jade gaining a B.A. degree in English. In 2006 together they started Convergence Church in the heart of inner city Atlanta, the highest crime rate zip code of the state of Georgia.

Due to this context, Jade has received first hand experiences in both middle class and impoverished black America. As College and Career pastors at a predominantly white Southern Baptist church, Corey and Jade have gained the privilege of providing insight into healthy racial integration. Roswell Street Baptist Church now has active members from 31 nationalities and services in 4 different languages. It is Jade's passion to see healing and understanding come to both black and white communities.